National History Series: USA

Chronicles of a Texas Pioneer

La Bahia Mission—Goliad

Chronicles of a Texas Pioneer

art and text by

Marie Love

The Stevenson Press

CALLCOTT-COLLINSON, INC.

Austin, Texas

Library of Congress Catalog Card No.: 78-12718
ISBN 0-89482-038-9 hardcover
ISBN 0-89482-039-7 softcover

Distributed by Southwest Book Services, 4951 Top Line Drive, Dallas, Texas 75247

In memory of my grandmother
Mrs. Mary Saphronia Love
for her sterling worth
and
her help to me in my shortcomings

Publisher's Note

The customs, conditions, and events described in this book are as they really were. Most of the people actually existed, although many of the names have been changed. The story takes place during the time the author's great-grandmother lived in Texas (from 1832). Although the events described are authentic, some of them did not actually take place in her great-grandmother's life, but happened to others who are not in the story. The dialog is, of course, fictionalized, although it has been kept true to the time.

At the time this story takes place, Texas was an outlying territory of Mexico, colonized predominantly by Anglo-Americans under grants such as that awarded to Stephen F. Austin. Mexico provided territorial government, but the colonists were largely left to govern themselves according to regulations made by the holders of the grants.

Relations between the settlements and Mexico began to deteriorate as the settlers became dissatisfied with Mexican law, imposed from such a distance and by a government that did not, therefore, seem aware of their needs. In meeting places such as Groce's Landing, a part of Groce's plantation on the Brazos River where there was a ferry and a trading center, the "Texicans" began to discuss Mexican statehood—the conservative suggestion—and independence—a radical new idea.

The settlers hoped relations would improve when Santa Anna, then supported by the colonies as a liberal candidate, was elected President of Mexico. After his election the political situation changed, however, and Santa Anna became determined to put down the Texas "insurrection." He began to gather an army just south of the Rio Grande River, and resentment grew until finally even Stephen F. Austin, the conservative, agreed to the bold step of declaring independence for the Republic of Texas.

Contents

Preface	ix
Prologue	3
Part One : The Beginnings	5
Part Two: Growth of Discontent	47
Part Three: The Runaway Scrape	69
Part Four: The Rebuilding	93
Epilogue	129

Preface

When I was about five years of age, my parents, Alonzo and Ida May Love, with their three small children, came to Grandma Saphronia Love's home in Texas to live during Dad's new school term. Dad was Grandma's son. We had been rushed in the move and had had no time to find another home.

Having the energy and curiosity of a usual child my age, I was always at Grandma's side—at the kitchen range, feeding the chickens, digging potatoes—even then marveling at her endurance, persistence, and knowledge, and the number of things that must wait for her attention. And I thought of her as being old even then.

Her parents, Jesse Brown and Margaret Patton Atkinson, had come to Texas with one of Stephen F. Austin's first groups of colonists in 1831. Mary Saphronia was born on February 13, 1838, at Washington-on-the-Brazos. Grandma Saphronia attended school at the Miller School for Young Ladies near the present town of Independence, Texas. Later, when she was about eighteen years of age, she taught in that school. Her family then lived near Gay Hill, and she rode to school each day on horseback. At the site of the Gay Hill home, an old log cabin—which had been her father's workshop—was the last landmark to disappear, in about 1968.

In 1858 Saphronia Atkinson married Dr. William Marshall Love, from Tennessee, who had come to Texas as a schoolteacher. He was also a minister of the Cumberland Presbyterian Church, having associated with Finis Ewing, one of the founders of that branch of Presbyterians. Dr. Love also went to New Orleans for a course of lectures in medicine which, when completed, granted him license to practice medicine. The school was the beginning of the Tulane Medical School.

In 1849, Dr. Love had joined a group that rode horseback (and muleback!) in the Gold Rush to California, becoming known as the "Forty-niners."

After their marriage, Dr. and Mrs. Love built their home near Yellow Prairie, now Chriesman in Burleson County. Dr. Love died soon after the Civil War, leaving his wife—with five small boys to care for, without the servants to which she had been accustomed in that day and in that part of the world, completely ignorant of the management of a home, especially cooking and sewing, and with none of the knowledge of the outside chores—to face alone the new dangers and trials of the postwar days.

But Grandma's stamina came to her support then, and grew as she used it. Also, her younger brother, Brown Atkinson, came to guide her in her new education and stayed with her through the darkest days. The two of them and the small boys managed to overcome the old problems, withstand the new ones, and survive the dangers.

Grandma Love died in the fall of 1927 in the home which she and her husband had established. She was almost eighty-nine years of age.

As I grew into womanhood, having followed my Dad as I had his mother, I knew of no work for a young lady to do other than teaching school. Dad thought a lady should remain in the home. Nevertheless, he helped me push myself through Normals and Teachers' Examinations. He himself had stopped teaching years before because of the toll taken by earlier hardships and the rigidly confining hours of the work.

I also had an unexpressed desire to be a writer, so, after ten years as a teacher, I came to Houston for a business course, later a B.B.A. degree. I contacted the *Houston Gargoyle*, a Houston magazine, with some success, but after two or three years its demise ended my writing career, too.

Then, for about twenty-five years, I was proud to hold the position of Deputy District Clerk in one of our district courts, a position then thought to be for men only!

When I retired, I thought, Now I can write! But all of my experiences seemed so ordinary and trite when put on paper.

Then I thought of my Grandma Saphronia!

But there I failed her. The story turned out to be the picture of the troubles and trials, customs and habits, positions and possessions of the times and days of pioneers and colonists. All that is true, as is the history. But as for the persons and families, much is fictionalized, or made up of composites, although much is also based upon truth.

M.L.
1978

Chronicles of a Texas Pioneer

Prologue

PIONEER DAYS ARE earthquakes that make mountains and lowlands from the plains of routine living. They lift ambitions to high peaks; they settle the strife involved in the turmoil of expansion and growth into peaceful valleys of content.

One is dependent upon the other for the completeness of its purpose, for the full glory of its existence. The people who play the roles in such development are puppets in the hands of a universal plan, but the manner in which the daily problems of living are performed is the pattern for the generations down through the years. The responsibility lies not lightly on any shoulder.

I am grateful for the pioneer spirit of our country called Texas. I am proud to be part and parcel of its being. My life is grounded into its prairies. My vision is bent toward its hills.

The vibrations—the hoofbeats of the advancing hordes of progress and the retreating forms of travail—resound in my ears.

In 1832, I came to Texas with my family during the first days of its colonization, accepting Stephen F. Austin's invitation to establish a homestead in its broad acreage of hills and prairies. Free land! And promises of a wide scope for living. Hardships! Perhaps, but those had been our daily experiences in Tennessee, too.

So I would take my young part in the trials and the progress of a new country.

But the sturdy inheritance that is mine is from the courage of my grandmother, Saphronia Bratton; the stalwart strength of my father, Andrew; and the whimsical humor of my Uncle Joseph—this inheritance was—and will be—my bulwark and my reserve.

I am now assuming new responsibilities and must prove that I am worthy of my family's gifts. But first, I want to record the experiences that have been ours—the life that makes a pioneer—both for my own help in the hard days ahead, and for those who may follow in my footsteps.

How memories crowd in!

I remember my first young adventure with romance.

A glance in the mirror hanging on my wall—in this year of 1838—brings a patronizing smile.

Part One

The Beginnings

1

I HAD GONE DOWN through our small pasture toward my favorite oak tree. There, while the changing sky formed a backdrop of opalesque colors, I repeated poems I loved and sang a song to the nightfall. It was my evening's program that summer when I was fifteen.

My path was the trail of the setting sun as it streamed through the branches of Texas oaks; my song was a duet with the mockingbirds, accentuated by the homing call of the dove.

But the path that evening suddenly lost its twilight peace and was fraught with danger. My song became a cry of fright as I saw the rattlesnake coiled for the strike. No sooner had my eyes focused on the menacing head and trembling fangs than the stillness was pierced by the crack of a pistol shot and the snake was writhing in the dust of the road. Another sound pulled my hypnotized gaze from the rattler and to a horse that bore his rider with swiftness and grace over the low rail fence of our pasture.

With the same ease, the rider dismounted and, sweeping his hat to the ground, said, "I hope my lady is not disturbed."

"Oh, no, I . . ." but evidently disturbed I was, for I folded up in a faint at his feet.

Consciousness came to me with the aid of Grandmother's smelling salts and her crisp voice. I opened my eyes only for a moment—some kind of caution advised closing them again.

"I assure you, Madam," the gentleman was saying, "I frightened her only by the shot with which I killed the rattler. It might have struck her in another moment and I—"

"Malinda knows how to handle rattlers," was my grandmother Bratton's astounding retort.

Why Grandma, I thought, I never killed one in my life!

I dared a peep through half-closed eyes and saw the young man, my rescuer, being hastened toward the door.

Grandmother softened her remark by adding, "But she evidently can't take to excitement, so thank you for bringing her home. And now, sir, good evening."

When she returned to my side my eyes were starry wide and many words were on my lips. She again astounded me by returning to our front door. Closing it, she dropped the heavy bar into place and stood my father's musket against the sill.

"Well, child, what happened?" she asked, too calmly.

"Oh, Grandma, it was a huge rattler, and isn't he handsome?"

"I did not see the rattler," she said, turning her head, and I thought her shoulder shook a bit.

"Oh, I did not mean the sn-a-a-k-e."

"I know, my dear, but the woods are full of both snakes and adventurers and if you will insist upon going down in that pasture late in the evening you will have to learn to cope with both. After all, Bossy would come in by herself if you hadn't spoiled her."

Bossy, our cow, was my very good excuse for the excursion which I loved so well.

Grandma continued, "Lie still while I get you some hot gruel. We'll probably not see this young troubadour again—but," she murmured to herself while bending over the steaming pot at our fireside, "there'll always be others."

I shivered, but not from fright. Not to see my newfound hero again? Glancing toward the door, astoundingly barred, and with my father's musket at the entrance to our cabin, I feared I never would. And I wondered why.

It was some time before I ventured down the trail again. But I missed my outings and felt I could not relinquish that which was my greatest pleasure in our simple life. So, with many admonitions on the part of Grandma, and with the understanding that she would call for me if I were not returned in due time, I was permitted to go.

One day I was startled to hear the hasty approach of a horse's hooves and was unable to move from fright and excitement. The white horse stopped short before me, bent his head and forelegs in a bow as his rider slid over his head to the ground. With a flourish of his arm as though removing a hat which he did not wear, the man stood with the horse in a long moment's tableau. I recognized my hero who had saved me from the rattlesnake and filled the woods with my relieved laughter. But suddenly I stopped and stood in embarrassed silence at my childish reaction.

My companion continued in the gallant characterization he had begun. "Malinda, what a lovely nymph you are! How truly you belong to the land of fairies and wood sprites!

"O dear Malinda Bratton,
"O charming Linda Bratton,
"There's ne'er flower that blooms in June
"That's half so fair as that one."

I knew that he was misquoting Burns but laughed gaily as he placed a light arm about my waist and danced me around and around the oak tree until I was breathless. As we leaned against the tree trunk in complete enjoyment, my eyes did not leave his face nor did he stop quoting poems one after another. And in most of them I could accompany him, as they were those I had read over and over from the books on our homemade shelves from Tennessee.

Suddenly the air was rent by the loud blast of a horn—my grandmother's call for me when she felt I should be in sight. The horn caused Bossy's calf to bellow and Bossy to respond and there was no further need of encouragement in her homegoing. If I were not in sight, too, Grandma would search for me. So I left my companion and ran rapidly down the trail, but, in appreciation of his astonishment and not wishing to appear rude, I turned to wave to him from the twist in the trail.

No later meeting was quite so exciting. During the days that followed I found my thoughts wandering to the twilight hours, wondering if my knight would be at our trysting place. And I did not yet know his name. But he knew mine! Remembering Grandma's reaction to his first appearance, I kept my thoughts to myself and dared not inquire of Father, or even Uncle Joe, as to the identity of this wandering knight without armor, our latest inhabitant of Hill Grande.

Grandma sent me to the trading post one morning to exchange our eggs and butter for some much-needed flour. When I had adjusted my sunbaked eyes to the contents of the darker room of the store, I saw my hero leaning against the homemade grocery counter, talking to Mr. Rogers. In my embarrassment, I turned to leave. Seeing the romantic figure in such an environment of real life left me unnerved and unhappy. Mixed with the homespun-clad figures of our neighbors, his fringed leather jacket, shiny boots, his long hair curling at his shoulders, seemed unreal; his personality not as appropriately placed as it was in the woody vale of our pasture. I did not wish to disturb my dream.

But Mr. Baker called to me and there was nothing to do but go forward with my errand. "Malinda, have you met our new schoolteacher, Mr. Brentwood Haynes?"

The bucket containing my exchange fell to the counter from nerveless fingers. I scarcely heard the remainder of Mr. Roger's introduction.

"Malinda will be one of your students, Mr. Haynes."

I thought, What will Grandma say now?

Brentwood Haynes assumed the responsibility of the moment with his usual ease. He found my hand on the counter where it lay limp and trembling, and bowing low over it, thereby hiding the wink he gave me, said, "And I can see that is going to be the greatest of pleasures."

Realizing my confusion he turned back to the counter and I covered my leave-taking the best I could. Out in the revealing sunlight again, I looked toward the small log room that was our schoolhouse and let large tears roll down my cheeks while I felt like laughing hysterically. I could not have told whether I were bitterly disappointed or divinely happy. I wondered if Grandma would permit me to have a part in such an instructor's program. Not if she knew all, I thought.

"But I shall hold it against you for failing to come to my rescue the other evening," a voice at my side startled me by saying.

I looked up at him, then gave a nervous glance down toward our cabin.

"But—I was in a faint!" I parried.

"Oh, then I only *thought* I saw those brown eyes open," he said. "Well, perhaps you will yet have the opportunity."

"I just can't believe you are a teacher!" Only wonder was in my voice.

"Neither can I," he laughed. "But it seems to fit into the program. Don't forget me, though, as a troubadour." I really was relieved when he vanished again into the dusk.

Hill Grande had very few school days and the leader for such teaching was necessarily one who could afford time from more pressing duties, hence usually the instructor was an old man who could not perform hard labor. There were no books other than those few volumes found on some pioneer's homemade shelves. Teaching consisted of reading from these books and lining off—for copying—such portions as were thought to be worthwhile or of need in the lives of the colony's settlers. Information was given in a general discussion, whether it were of a mathematical problem or of some question of daily living. Many times the adults of the group completely absorbed the time allotted to the program and young children slipped out of the room unnoticed to go about their outside games. With such a program, schoolteachers could make the daily work to their liking or knowledge. Perhaps Brentwood Haynes would teach only poetry! I would be pleased with that.

Although I read and studied at home under Grandma's and Uncle Joe's tutoring, Father would want me to be a part of such a neighborly undertaking as was the school, when one was available. He carefully took a part in all of the affairs of our settlement and usually was the leader by common consent. Did he have any part in choosing Brentwood as our teacher?, I wondered. Walking slowly home, digging my homemade shoes through the sand of our only village roadway, I pondered that there was nothing else to be done in view of Bratton principles. I would have to face my schoolteacher each day as though there might not be future romantic meetings under my oak tree. And I fervently hoped that there would be other meetings!

When school opened I was a member of the group assembled in the tiny room. No mention of the struggle which had preceded my grandmother's consent had come to my ear, but I felt the tenseness of the atmosphere in our family circle, the silence which met my prattle about school and its activities. I began to feel embarrassed and hesitant in mentioning the common household subject. I felt childish and meek. Was I to become a problem to my family? In the schoolroom Brentwood Haynes treated me as any other pupil of his class. Of course he had to, but sometimes I was furious. Only under the oak tree did I feel natural.

One evening I stood beneath the tree and shaded my eyes from the glancing rays of the setting sun. As I watched, and waited, I saw the horse and then its rider as he pushed aside the low branches of the underbrush. Brentwood rode with a precision as though deep in thought. It was so unlike his usual mien, and there was only a few minutes in which to learn of his preoccuption. But the poem was there, the song rang out, and he whistled the last bar as he pressed my hand. I felt there was more he would say.

"Queen Mab, someone wants copying done and I shall have to be away for a while. Please let the school folk know. And if I were you, I'd not be too far from home." His voice trailed away and he looked about as though trying to memorize the surroundings. My eyes showed my concern, I suppose, as he pinched my cheek and said, "Oh, there is nothing to worry about, really. I shall just not be around to keep the dragons away."

"I was not concerned for myself, Brentwood," I said. "I am not afraid. You know, I think Neleetah actually keeps guard over us."

Neleetah was our usually unseen Indian friend. Too old to keep up with his wandering tribe, he had chosen our neighborhood to settle down in.

"Yes," Brentwood said absently. "But I was not thinking of the Indians, either. But I do expect to see you again before you hardly miss me."

He was up on his horse and away, singing, "Malinda, mio, what are you thinking of?"

The call to other settlements to do copying of important letters, orders, and messages was not a new one. Brentwood was one of the few who could go about and give such service legibly and quickly. He wrote a beautiful script. So the call for hasty copying did not upset me so much as his abstracted manner. To what new adventure was he going?

2

SCHOOL WAS intermittent, but real.

"And what battle was fought in Europe on June 15, 1815, Miss Bratton?"

A leafy branch of the old oak tree filled an opening in the ragged roof of the tiny room used for our school. I pulled my languid eyes from its intrigue and found the voice below. But I had expected the half-mocking, half-teasing face of my lover. Instead, the frown was purely that of a pedagogue. My face burned. I was not so undone from embarrassment as I was from anger. Brentwood Haynes had no right to take me so unaware. However, a paper brushed my hand on the roughly hewn bench and I had only to glance down at it to read the answer scribbled on it.

"Why, Waterloo, was it not?"

The silence was deafening.

"Yes, but to the loss of what country?"

That answer, too, was on the paper.

"France!" I almost shouted in victory.

The questions passed on to others. I was more at attention but our teacher knew that I was not interested in history nor any of the duller facts of life. I wanted only poetry, grammar, and diagraming, the things I hoped to teach in the girls' seminary which the settlement expected to have in the near future. Father planned that I would complete my education in Tennessee and return to the settlement at Hill Grande when the seminary was established. I had definite ideas about what I would want to teach. History was my difficult subject and Brentwood Haynes had learned of my aversion to it. I would have found school hours very dull and hardly worth the use of time valuable in home duties except that I found him the most exciting person! Especially when he quoted long passages of poetry, when he broke into spells of patriotic dramatization, when he led us in the ballads of the day. Then I was all attention. Now I wonder if he did not find the incentive to continue those long discourses in the complete adoration reflected in my eyes! I was willing to accept the reprimand which now and then he deemed necessary to bestow upon me. I thought it might conceal the fact that my thoughts were chiefly of the possibility of another rendezvous at the old oak tree where I might continue my beloved poetry with him.

Red-haired Steve Adkins walked home with me almost every afternoon, as he took his mother buttermilk from Grandmother's small barrel churn.

"Thank you, Steve, for coming to my rescue. I never would have remembered that battle. How do you manage the answers so readily?"

Steve dug a bare toe in the sand, then raised it to remove the sandbur before replying.

"Oh, he gave us that one yesterday. I write them down. And I could see you were about half-asleep."

"No, not asleep, but dreaming with my eyes open," I laughed, then tagged him for the run to the house.

Steve had come to my rescue so often I was afraid he might be discovered and punished for his help. Brentwood was a tall man and could see over our heads although the benches were grouped closely in the tiny room. But I helped Steve, too, in the evenings, especially with hard diagraming. He just did not remember poetry very well and paraphrasing was as hard for him as history and mathematics might be for me.

I lost the race to the house because I suddenly remembered that Grandma said it was not becoming for a young lady to run races. So I was still walking to the door and catching my breath when Steve came out drinking buttermilk from a gourd dipper and carrying a pail of it.

"Muscadines getting turned," he said, "and those wild grapes will soon be just right for your grandma's jelly."

"Won't get much done till after the camp meeting, though," Grandma came to the door to answer. "Have to get something in the way of food ready to take there first. We might pick the grapes the last day of the meeting and do them when we get home."

Grandma was noted throughout the settlement for her grape jellies, preserves, and wine. She could do wonders with honey and muscadines. She knew the best dyes of the woods about us and we always laid in a supply of rutabaga toothbrushes—a root that kept for some time and made a good toothbrush whether one used the tobacco snuff or not. So our autumn trips to the woods were veritable harvesting adventures.

Grandma was a typical pioneer. When, in 1832, her two sons decided to go west, to Texas, she declared that it could not be rougher than her early days in Tennessee, and she had no hesitancy in accompanying them. Grandma, Father, and Uncle Joe were my family. I did not remember my mother. But I was not to be pampered because of that. Grandma had given me many punishments with a peach-tree switch; Father had only to gather me in his arms and I would repent and burst into tears; and Uncle Joe did not need to utter a word if I had committed a misdemeanor in his presence—his silence was more impressive than a scolding. Yet I cannot remember having been afraid of them, my family. My acts were always of a mischievous nature, wholly without premeditation. My tears too often were from a spirit of defeat rather than of repentance. But seldom did I succeed in avoiding the hour of discovery. For that reason I thoroughly enjoyed my clandestine meetings with Brentwood and appreciated the fact that it was our secret.

"What did you say your religion is, Linda?" Steve asked me again. He never would say "Malinda" in full.

"Cumberland Presbyterian," and I spelled it for him. "My grandfather was a preacher. But we don't say much about it here, you know, as every colonist that comes to Texas is supposed to be Catholic. I don't know why anyone cares. But we just didn't happen to be, and, besides, there is no Catholic church, nor preacher."

" 'Priest,' you mean," corrected Steve, whose mother was Catholic. "Yes, I know. So we all go to the camp meeting instead. Will your grandmother shout again this year?"

"Steve, be ashamed! That is a very sacred—uh—rite." I hesitated. I hardly knew what it might be called but Grandma did often shout when she heard the old songs. Her happy, glorified face inspired others and the preacher then knew that a good revival was beginning. I was always embarrassed by remarks of some of the critical. But when Father heard them he would rise up in all his great dignity and, with such a look of power and true belief about him, all thought of ridicule was banished, with either fear or religion taking its place.

"Well, Mother says she wishes she was well enough to go but even if I could get her there she would not enjoy the preachin.' "

"Say '*were* well enough,' Steve." I did not mean to offend him nor show off any superior knowledge but rather wished to help. It was just part of my training for schoolteaching.

"Well, 'was' or 'were,' it's time for me to get about home," and Steve, with the speed of a deer, balancing the full bucket of milk on his shoulder, ran out of sight down the dusty road that bordered the homes of the settlement. He and his mother lived down near the trading post.

"Malinda, don't forget to see about the candles and tapers before you go after the cow," Grandma called from indoors as I lingered at the doorstep, throwing out shelled corn to the fluttering hens about me. Father planned building a chicken house soon.

"Yes, Grandma."

Grandma and I made candles once a week but it was my duty before nightfall to see that the stubs placed about the house were long enough to last through the evening and would do for any emergency which might arise. Then I was supposed to make the tapers—out of newspaper if we were fortunate to have some about the place—or corn husks, rolling them into tight little rolls and placing them in the broken pottery pitcher by the fireplace, where they would be easy to find.

3

HILL GRANDE WAS a well-established community of some half-dozen families when my father, grandmother, Uncle Joe, and I arrived in 1832. Father liked the rolling hills and lovely valleys. When the two oxen-drawn wagons halted under the massive oak trees, it was in silent, mutual consent that this spot was approved as our future home. There had been many weary days of travel from Tennessee, many problems to overcome as mile after mile of uncut road was followed by the wagon train of which we were a part, many homesick hours, and many misgivings, all of which made this landing a happy one and the small dot of human habitation a haven indeed. For several days we rested under the oak trees or wandered about the vast acres that were my father's and Uncle Joe's portion of the great unimproved lands of Texas. We stored up sunshine in weary muscles, and enthusiasm for a new life in weary minds.

The settlement had a small fort in it, with a two-storied lookout. This height, added to that of the hill upon which it was built, gave a wonderful view over the countryside. There was also a small trading post where we might find rare food and clothing for a few hours after a wagon train had arrived from Groce's Landing. The Groce family's Liendo Plantation was at Groce's Landing, and a ferry crossed the Brazos River there, which was how a wagon train sometimes came our way. But we had laid in a goodly store of food before leaving Louisiana on the last lap of our own trip, so with Grandma's careful planning we fared well that first winter.

Father and Uncle Joe had soon begun to fell the trees, medium size, all as nearly alike as possible, to build our home. Some of the other settlers had helped because it was the neighborly custom, but everyone was so busy with his own new home that Father and Uncle Joe had asked assistance only in laying the logs in place after the ends had been prepared, cleat and notch, to fit in proper joining. We had no roof until the woodwork and blacksmith shop, which was to be our livelihood, had been established.

My father was a powerful man and lifted logs and pulled rocks about the place with the mighty arm of his forty years. Uncle Joe was small and, having followed his older brother about all of his life, usually waited to help rather than to lead out. He was Grandma's baby. Not having had a daughter, and also having been left a widow when her boys were mere youths, Grandma had mothered Uncle Joe and had tried to shield him from the harder things of life, even to the point of doing them herself. I was too small to be of much assistance, but Grandma lifted and bent with as much ability as the men. The heavier work, however, always fell upon Father, and I can realize now that the responsibility made him a stronger man, both physically and intellectually.

The long hours and steady toil made weary muscles and stiff joints in sixteen-year-olds as well as in those of adult years, and we welcomed the cool nights when sleep made all renewed in its relaxing oblivion. The music of the katydids was unheeded; the cry of the coyote, or the pack from which he had grown apart, was only one of the night's heartbeats. Labor and success, slumber and rest, was the song of our daily program.

Months passed. Before the first heavy frost, and long before the first cold Texas northers began to blow, we were comfortably settled in our first home—two rooms, or cabins, joined by a long open hall, or dogtrot, and with the rooms opening onto the dogtrot. A lean-to at the back was used for storage. The windows had shutters made from split timber, and hung on wooden hinges. For some time we had not felt the need for actual doors in our doorways.

But one morning when Grandma arose as usual, about five o'clock, to begin the early breakfast, she heard a noise on the dogtrot. Looking toward the door space of our room she saw a bear standing in the opening. Father had robbed a bee tree the day before and there was quite an aroma of honey about the place. Grandma was rather accustomed to the traits of the bear in Tennessee and as soon as she recovered from the shock of seeing the visitor, she realized what the bear wanted. She called to Father, who crawled out of the window, got a pan of the honey from the storeroom, and enticed the bear out by placing it under a tree some yards from the house. No one had the heart to shoot such a homing bear, so, after finishing the repast, our bruin shuffled off into the forest, probably to a family down in the thicket.

We had doors with bars for fastenings before nightfall.

The hillsides had many rocks jutting out of the embankments. Father and Uncle were able to quarry enough of them to build a beautiful chimney and fireplace before the second winter. However, our first fireplace was made with rocks around the base only, and the chimney was constructed with wood chunks and clay daubs from the creek bed. Our floors were of hewn timber, rough at first but partly covered with skin rugs—which kept splinters from my bare feet. Father made our furniture as he found the time to spare from more pressing problems. He and Uncle Joe slept on beds built into the walls of the house. This was done by sticking poles into the cracks between the logs before the walls were completed. The poles stuck out into the room, and two jointed limbs of a green sapling were then driven into the dirt floor to support the sticking-out ends of the poles. Then crosspieces held up the mattress. This was the usual settlement bed. Some time passed before we had raised sufficient corn to have shuck mattresses. They seemed cleaner than the moss-filled ones but were no softer. Father said hard mattresses had made a man out of many a weakling.

Grandma had brought her bed and feather mattress from Tennessee. Father made a trundle bed for me. This bed was pushed under Grandma's high-slatted one during the day and left our room free for daily living. Cooking was done in that room, about the huge fireplace. The crane hanging from its chimney bar was ever the bearer of a steaming pot of water. The iron Dutch oven stood ready to bake bread, potatoes, or meat when the hot coals and ashes were banked under and over its blackened form. Our fuel was huge logs from the forests with chips from Father's planing block. Food was a tedious art, a constant chore, a challenging privilege, but the result was most often a source of great pride. It was life to the pioneer woman, and her satisfaction in meeting the needs of her family with the work of her hands and the gifts of the soil was one of her major contributions to the times.

Our meat was wild turkey, squirrel, rabbit, and venison. Father and Uncle Joe were good at hunting. One winter we shared a buffalo with some neighbors, for any surplus was passed on to others or had to be dried on the walls of our storeroom. We had a smokehouse the second winter, which helped in preserving our supply.

Honey and sorghum molasses were used as long sweetening. It was the second year of our residence at Hill Grande that the settlers established the sugar mill. Father constructed it out of some scrap iron. The neighbors secured a huge caldron in which the syrup was cooked.

Although the supply of sugarcane was not great, the slow process and the slower tread of the oxen turning the mill made the sugar-making season a test to the patience of busy men. Children vied with one another in trying to help feed the mill, but only proved to be more in the way, and their toll in the sugarcane consumed made such assistance an expensive one. But the products were good. The crystalized part was used for sugar, and the syrup—and even the dregs, or darker portion, called "blackstrap"—was in demand. And sugar was one of the rare products of our pioneer days.

Grandma used the finely sifted ashes from our fire and the refuse tallow, or grease from the neighbor's hog-killings, to make a very good laundry soap. This soap she traded for chickens or other produce from the neighbors and the trading post. Almost everything was arranged by trade. Through such means, Father obtained our cow, some iron to make tools, and corn seed for the first spring planting.

Grandma also earned the reputation for being the doctor for the settlement. Grandfather had been a doctor as well as a preacher and we had many of his medical books with us. Grandma referred to them avidly but had some difficulty at first with the malaria and chills and fever of our settlement. However, she studied all that also, and soon learned the use of quinine. Whiskey was used by almost everyone for every ailment—especially was it kept handy for snakebites. Tobacco juice was a quick cure for a bee sting, and soda packs were cures not to be taken lightly. Grandma made a concoction which we called "homemade salve," for lack of a scientific name. It consisted of tallow or other oils, turpentine, and melted gum camphor. When these were heated, a bit of laudanum was added. The mixture congealed to the consistency of the oil used and was a very good cure for sprains, cuts, colds, chilblains, and any other ailment of either man or beast—if taken with due faith! We used it for sore throats and sore muscles alike and our home was a dispensary for it at all hours of the day.

Self-preservation was the duty of every Texan and the greatest of the dangers were not the Indians. No doctor could be had without many miles and hours—even days—of travel, during which time death often became the victor. Grandma's early days, and Grandfather's books, had prepared her in a great measure to meet this need.

Father was frequently called upon to make coffins for the dead. During the early months these crude boxes were made of the unplaned lumber that he and Uncle Joe were able to hew from the great trees of our forest during their spare time. But later they worked to have on hand some of the beautiful walnut or oak, planed in shiny surface and showing the grain of the wood in lovely patterns. Grandma and I often padded the inside of the box with moss from the trees, covering it with any cloth that might be obtained; especially was this thought necessary for women and children.

Now and then a call came from someone so far away that the work had to be done throughout the night. Father learned the advantage of having the candle near his work and found that I could be trusted to hold the light—not too near Uncle Joe's long hair, not too close to Father's bald pate. During these night sessions I learned the stories of the countryside. Some of them were so exciting that my imaginative mind created horrible dreams from them when I went to my little trundle bed. But because of the unusual news and excitement the stories brought, and because I loved being near my father, I would not leave my post. Often the narrative became too rough for my presence and then Father would not permit me to remain. Especially was that true when the stories of combat began to prevail. Those I devoured with all the fervor of a true pioneer. *Book* history might not be easy for me to remember, but in this new frontier *our* history was being made—or so said the narrator—and I was in the midst of it. And *our* history I could not forget!

One night my candle flickered and went out. I had accidentally snuffed it out with the only long breath I had taken for minutes. Father was worried about my presence this night—he had grown increasingly so, lately, although I wasn't sure why—but it was a rush job, so I gave him a smile, found another candle, and stuck to my post. The work was on the box that would hold the body out in front of the shop—the still body of a man who had been killed trying to prevent the confiscation of a load of corn he was taking to Groce's Landing to exchange at the plantation for money or trade. That corn would have been his winter's living.

Two neighbors had brought him in.

"As I figure it," said the spokesman, a rough-appearing fellow whose voice trembled, "some scamp had laid a trap in the road by spreading branches of the brush over a pit he had dug in the downhill grade of that winding trail to the La Bahia. The oxen's legs were broke. And it wasn't the work of no Indian, 'cause no Indian would use a sorry arrer like that 'un."

"Arrow?" asked Father as he raised up to take a better slant on the work before him.

"Yep, the arrer that kilt Mr. Roan. He must've started down the road expectin' to spend the night gettin' help, but, hearin' a noise, turned back to his waggin and was shot through the heart. A purty good shot, if'n the rascals was at the waggin, as he were about fifty yards away layin' on his face and the arrer jammed clean through him by his fall.''

''Who found him?'' asked Uncle Joe.

''Wal, *we* did.'' He inclined his head toward the door, where the other neighbor stood. ''His wife didn't git worried till the third or fourth day. Gosh! The waggin was there, empty, corn shucks spread aroun', and the animals looked like they had started to skin 'em and got scared off. It was awful.''

''We buried the ox in the trap and rushed here,'' spoke the other man. ''Someone's got to tell Mrs. Roan, yet. Sho 'nuff it ain't the work of no Indian. More'n two of us had better to go tell his widder. It's a good twenty mile, nearly halfway to La Grange. She's safe enough but we who go tell her'll probably be watched.''

It was late afternoon the next day when the caravan returned. Four men on horses came into the settlement and were followed by Father in our wagon, which was piled high with household effects. The other passengers were the widow, Mrs. Roan, and her two children.

A house-raising for the new inhabitants of the settlement, the Roan widow and her children, was the proper and neighborly act. Everyone joined in the plans. Haste was necessary as it was difficult to find extra room for anyone. Father and Uncle Joe slept in the hall on a pallet until the house was completed, relinquishing their bunks to the bereaved family. The women cooked large supplies of food—cornbread, sweet potatoes and pumpkins, turnip greens, and corn—and spread dinner under the trees, picnic fashion. I carried large pots of black coffee and water to the working men. The forest rang with the sound of ax upon wood, of trees crashing to the ground, bringing the smaller ones in their paths down with them. The men shouted to each other in friendly ballyhoo and made merriment of the hard labor. The work progressed rapidly.

Three brothers and their old father had come to give their aid. It was good to have the strong young arms of the brothers. They worked steadily and with little wasted effort, seeming to be trained in the work of hewing timber. Their name was Ryan. No one knew where they lived. The brothers were often seen about the trading post but they seldom joined in the usual activities of the other men. They rode mustang ponies, Indian style, and it was thought their livelihood was in horse-trading. Their father was morose and retiring. Any effort to break through their reserve during the house-raising met with a stolid resistance.

The widow Roan, a thin woman with pale high cheeks and black hair that accentuated her pallor, seemed very grateful for the friendliness shown to her in her emergency. She tried to be helpful but left the plans for her future home entirely with her new neighbors, seeming to be impassive as to her needs. She cried a great deal and talked for long hours with Grandma and the other women, but did not show her emotions in the presence of the men nor her own children. The boy, Jim, about seven years of age, and Jane, "going on five," as she put it, were frightened and timid. Winning them to the new setting of their life and trying to assure them of our good wishes was the chief diversion of Uncle Joe and myself each evening. Jim responded fairly readily, but Jane was cross and fretful and for a while would not be pleased. But Uncle Joe used the tricks and jokes with which he had beguiled me for many hours, and since no one could withstand his twinkling eyes and his witty remarks he completely won over the children, and I found we two were more or less encumbered with their care.

Only three days were required to complete the house and move in their family. Estelle Roan wore her widow's black even though it was the heavy black of her winter wardrobe and the summer was hot and sultry. But a house-raising was not complete without a housewarming.

More food was cooked—someone killed some wild turkeys—and we gathered about the tiny house and had a feast. Brentwood was there to lead in the songs we sang. A suggestion was made that everyone be required to do something for entertainment. Uncle Joe danced a jig, Father blew through his fist to make music. Grandma recited the Twenty-third Psalm and led in prayer. Brentwood quoted a poem about the home. I could not think of anything that would be different, so I asked Grandma, Father, and Uncle Joe to join in singing the "Hunter's Horn" round, which we had sung together from the time I could first remember. Grandfather was a Scotchman and the old Scotch melody was a compelling one. I could remember how proud I was when I was first able to carry a tremulous part. So there in the shadows of our new neighbor's home, with the only light about us from the stars and the fireflies, we sang our roundelay.

Before the words escape my memory, I want to put them down here. I think we have not sung it since that long-ago night in September.

The Hunter's Horn

The hunter winds his bugle horn,
"To horse! To horse! Hallo! Hallo!"
The fiery courser snuffs the morn
And thronging serfs their lords pursue.

The eager pack from couples freed
Dash through the bush, the brier, the brae,
While answering hound and horn and steed
Resounding echoes startling wake.

Up springs from yonder tangled thorn
A deer more white than mountain snow,
And louder rings the hunter's horn—
"Hark, forward! Forward! Hallo! Hallo!"

I even now cannot recall the next verse, but I'm glad—as I cannot think of that beautiful deer being slaughtered.

4

WAGON AFTER WAGON rolled into its accustomed place about the campmeeting grounds at Dripping Springs. Families who had come on previous years had their favorite spots and trouble would have ensued if anyone else had presumed to usurp these ''rightful'' places. New families took spots on an outer circle and perhaps were more fortunate in having a little more privacy, although less protection. The covered wagons provided dressing rooms and sleeping quarters for the ladies. The men took the hard ground for sleep, and a pillow or blanket, if they were so fortunate as to possess one. The meeting often lasted two weeks and seldom did one group remain throughout its session. There were always leavetakings and welcomes intermingled with other social and religious activities of the day. Early September was the chosen time for the gathering, as the weather might be too chilly later in the fall. But often the cotton had not been gathered or the corn sold, so the men brought their families, stayed a few days, then returned home to carry on the work of the farmer. Seldom did a family have horses to use in their transportation and the oxen team would be needed back at home. Sufficient protection, however, against possible Indian raids and wild animals roaming the thicket necessitated a large number of men on the grounds.

The old arbor used for shelter during preaching services was broken down in many places and had to be repaired. Branches of trees were placed upon new pole rafters, making a fragrant, cool covering from sun and showers alike. Seats were made by rolling logs into convenient places, or some of them were split, and laid from one tree stump to another. Women and children usually preferred the pallets made from their nighttime coverings—skins or blankets.

The only light was that from the circle of campfires about the enclosure, and these also furnished cooking facilities and heat for the chilly nights. An aroma of frying meat, sweet potatoes baking in the ashes, or bread in the large iron skillets, filled the air, "whetting the appetites," as the men would say after their outdoor exercise. Grandma had a favorite dish that she always baked and passed around, hot and appetizing. This "johnnie cake," as it was called, was made of cornmeal, milk, eggs, and molasses. It was not quite a cake, nor yet cornmeal, but was truly food fit for a king. It gave her the entree she desired to meet new people and to renew acquaintances with old friends.

It was at the camp meeting that I met Sophie Ryan. I know now that a new era opened in my life that day. There had been few girl companions of my childhood and there were no young ladies in our settlement. Sophie was older than I and she was married, but there was the young look about her that touched Grandma's heart. We found her alone with her horse tied to a tree, a skillet in her hand, and a blanket spread on the ground. I grasped the full skirt of Grandma's dress and pointed.

"Look, Grandma!"

"Mm," was all Grandma said, but we went over to Sophie.

"Welcome, child. Are you all alone?"

"Yes'm," said Sophie.

"Malinda and I would like to have you over near our wagon, if you like. I think you would find it more comfortable and companionable over there."

Sophie's eyes grew moist. "Oh, thank you, Ma'am, but I guess I'd better not."

"Why, poof, of course you'd better. Have you ever spent the night down here? The noises might be frightening to you if you haven't."

"Are your people coming later?" I ventured to ask.

Sophie's mouth set in a hard line as she said flatly, "No."

Grandma and I looked at each other, and then she said, "Well, I'll have to be gettin' back to camp. Malinda, stay awhile to keep her company. But don't stay too long. There'll be prayer meeting at sundown, you know."

I had momentarily forgotten that age-old custom but nodded now in remembrance and said, "Yes'm, Grandma."

I settled down on the ground with Sophie. "I am Malinda Bratton and that is my grandma, Saphronia Bratton."

"I am Sophie Ryan. I guess you've heard of me." Bitterness was in her voice. I truly was astonished, because I *had* heard of her, and could hardly suppress the exclamation. "Oh!" I modified it by adding, "Of course. I have wanted to meet you but wondered if I ever would."

And that was true, although I had no idea she was so young and so pathetically beautiful. She was the only woman of the Ryan family. One seldom spoke of the woman. Although she and her husband, Johnnie Ryan, lived apart from the old father and the other two brothers, the names of the sons and the old man were connected in many stories, fanciful and otherwise, mostly involving crime. We had wondered about them at the house-raising. But I could see that this woman was not one of them, whether she lived with them or not. She was unhappy.

My excited questions came out. I was glad for an opportunity to learn about her. What state was her home? How long had she been married? She had come from Missouri and from a lonely father and mother. To my last question she answered, "About six months."

"Oh, I've always wanted to see a wedding!" I exclaimed.

To my surprise she burst into tears. "There was no wedding! I ran away!"

As the sun hid its face behind the old oak forest, Sophie poured out her story, which had been held within her so long that the telling of it was like the breaking of an embankment during a flood. She had met Johnnie Ryan at her home in Missouri, where he had come with a herd of mustang ponies. She had been overwhelmed by his passionate declarations of love and his stories of Texas. Although her parents had fought her marriage to him with intensity and earnestness, she had run away with Johnnie. So swift were his horses and so thorough his knowledge of byways, that they were out and away before her parents could have missed her.

All down the rugged trail, Sophie had asked for, searched for, a preacher, so they could be married. She was tired, but happy and thrilled, with no doubts or anxieties. She was in love. But Texas preachers or officers of the law were not to be found, and she and Johnnie had arrived at Hill Grande and he had introduced her to his family as his wife, with a huge wink and a kiss for Sophie.

She was too embarrassed and timid, before the frowns of disapproval of the father and the sneers of the boys, to voice a denial. She had clung to Johnnie in fright. He had stood by her at all times and defended her in many issues. He had built their little home with his own hands, as his brothers refused to help. They had wanted a woman, they said, to cook for them. The father had remained silent. He definitely did not want a woman around, and neither did he want to be deprived of the supporting help of his oldest son. There were many fights and quarrels, during all of which Sophie had stayed in her little one-room cabin and tried to adjust to the way she knew she must live. She still loved Johnnie, and she tried to bring his thinking around to her ideas of a husband and wife, to persuade him to have a marriage ceremony, even if by an officer of the law.

"And now," Sophie's tears broke out afresh, "I am expectin'."

"Expectin'?" I did not know what she meant and searched her face, taking her hands, wet with her tears, into mine and drying them on my homespun skirt. "What—is that, Sophie?"

The look she gave me was almost of horror. Then she burst into nervous laughter and her tiny body shook with her sobs. I did not then know the symptoms of hysteria, so I merely held her hands tightly in mine as new emotions engulfed me. But suddenly she stopped, and, looking into my astonished face, must have realized that I was not ridiculing her but spoke in earnest.

"A child, Innocence," she said, then kissed my hands that held hers. "And I do want one, but not like this! Not until I am really married! Oh, you are so sweet and lovely, you must know how to help me. Johnnie would not come down here, said he could not stand such rigamarole, but I need prayer, I do need help." Now her tears were streaming down her face. I could not doubt her sincerity.

"And you'll get it, don't worry! There is a way and we'll find it. But look, it is time for prayer meeting. Come on and we'll talk tomorrow."

"Only don't tell your grandmother yet," she begged.

"Of course not," I replied quickly. She did not know how straitlaced my Grandma Saphronia was.

People were already gathering for the prayer meeting. The women were in one group and fortunately were near us, so we slipped into place just as Grandma began her first prayer. The men gathered in another group far enough away so that one assembly would not disturb the other. I was quite sure that Father would be chosen to lead the men. In the two years we had attended the meetings, Grandmother and Father had become leaders. Grandma's prayers were long. When she closed she asked for others, but if none came she began to sing, and that was easier for me. This time, especially, it was hard to jump right from the experience I had just had and into beginning to pray for the good of my soul. And I could not bring Sophie's secret out in public. But I could sing, though my mind was in turmoil.

I realized I knew very little about babies. I could not remember being around a small child as we had no babies in the settlement. Once I had asked Grandma some questions but she only said, "Sh! child, that is not for your young years. You will know that in good time," which filled my mind with mysteries and only increased my curiosity. But there had been no occasion with all our pioneer problems to bring up such a subject again. If I asked questions regarding our early family life Grandma would motion for me to cease and later would tell me that my father's heart was broken when my mother died and that it would be best not to discuss it. I had thought that parenthood was an eternal thing, and that it grew out of marriage. Now to know the story of a runaway, who did not get married but was going to have a baby, disturbed the very depths of my soul.

Prayer meeting finally ended, and Sophie and I stood hand in hand, whispering until Grandma found us.

''Children, come on to supper. Malinda, I think your friend will enjoy some johnnie cake. It should be done by now.''

I did not realize how timid a young woman could be made to feel after months of a life such as Sophie had described. She ate of the food, but excused herself soon after and ran like a frightened deer back to her camp. Grandma just looked after her, then watched my perplexed face.

''Well, just leave her be,'' she advised. ''But when the wolves begin to howl tonight, I am worried for her.''

''But she will be at the preachin','' I said.

After tidying up the place I sat out under the trees to watch for my new friend. She came and we went and sat by Grandma's side as quiet as two babes in the woods during the opening of our camp meeting. The preacher was Methodist. He had just established a church at Bastrop and was on his way back through the settlements, holding meetings during the fall season. There had been a real church established in East Texas, but that was far away from our home. We always welcomed any preacher, and, as Grandma said, Methodist and Cumberland Presbyterians were very much alike. The Presbyterians had sent several preachers about the settlements but our particular church had not yet sent a man out to Texas.

We learned that the widow Roan was Methodist. She had come down to the camp meeting along with us, and Uncle Joe drove her wagon while Father drove ours. Since there was no space conveniently near us, Grandma had asked Mrs. Roan to join us for the noon meal. It made quite a picnic and the children enjoyed eating out. Before many days of such close companionship, however, Grandma began to regret that she had been so hospitable. The widow had taken a fancy to Uncle Joe, and I thought that he in turn accepted the chores necessary to her welfare at such an outing with all the grace of a man who was head of his house. He fed her oxen, gathered wood for her fires, cared for the children, and saw that water was plentiful in her water bucket that was hanging on the wagon tree. I heard Grandma talking to Father about it.

"Joe's just the type she would pick on," she said, "I wish I had never seen her."

Father did not remind Grandma that Uncle Joe was about the only person the widow could choose. An unmarried man in the settlement was a rare thing, and it might be the general opinion that if there were a man without a family, he should take unto himself the care of such a needy one as the widow Roan's. I thought it might be a wonderful thing if they fell in love.

My Uncle Joe was very emotional. Preachers holding the camp meetings soon learned to play upon his deep religious convictions and sentimental reactions. They preached, warning of "hell and eternal punishment," and watched as Uncle Joe's lips trembled and his eyes filled with tears. They talked louder and more earnestly for repentance of sins and bent accusing fingers at his bowing head. It made me very indignant. If Uncle Joe had ever committed a sin I was sure it was not of record. But invariably Grandma began to shout in this proceeding and others joined in the rejoicing. I felt only relief, and was sure that Grandma wanted undue attention turned away from her son.

Such excitement did not begin before the second or third night. It took some time for everyone to get settled down to the real purpose of the gathering. Happenings of the year were discussed—current news of politics, Indian raids, and crops gathered and to be gathered. Women exchanged ideas and gossip. One woman brought her cotton to be carded and taught others who had not known of such an art. Before she went home, her cards had been spoken for by a dozen or more women who needed them. Grandma already had cards and a spinning wheel. By the third year in our home in Texas, in the little field enclosed by a split-rail fence built by Father and Uncle Joe, enough cotton was grown to make us much-needed cloth—clothes and covering for our threadbare beds.

After the meeting, campfires were rebuilt for the night and to supply the morning's fire. Smoke hung low and heavy under the trees. One by one the campers retired. I could not sleep but lay with my new thoughts, so earnestly delving into the seriousness of them that I did not realize anything unusual was transpiring until someone called from the opening of our wagon cover.

"Malinda, are you there?"

Grandma stirred. "Who is it?"

But I was already at the opening.

"It's me, Mrs. Bratton—Sophie. I can't stand the howl of those wolves another minute!"

"Bless you, my child, of course you shouldn't. They won't come near so many fires, but you should not be out there alone. Crawl in here by Malinda."

Grandma was soon snoring again. I lay very still by Sophie but could not let myself touch her. "She is with child. . ." I did not know all of what that meant. But I remembered my Bible lessons. I repeated the reassuring verses over and over and said my prayers again and again until finally I fell asleep.

I was so engrossed in Sophie's troubles that it did not occur to me that I had not yet seen my own lover, Brentwood, among the campers. Although school was held only during the warm months because of lack of heating and comfortable quarters, it was more or less adjourned for the camp-meeting season. The second day I saw Brentwood's tall figure among the men grouped under the arbor and, seeing Father and Uncle Joe, I ran toward them without thought of embarrassment. The silence that fell upon my approach was noticeable, but Brentwood quickly covered it by calling, "And now comes a reminder of my chief occupation, gentlemen—schoolteaching!"

Father's frown stopped me, however, and I said, "Oh!"

"Come, my child," said my kindly father. "Mr. Haynes was just bringing us some important news. Austin has returned from Mexico."

"How wonderful!" I exclaimed, and wondered that the news had not brought more happy response from the men. Father told me later that plans to organize against the further invasion of the Mexican army were inevitable. Also, he said, my hero, Austin, favored establishing Texas as a separate Mexican state and returning to the Constitution of 1824. But there were many hard feelings, and there had been many skirmishes, and many other Texans just wanted to be Texas and not a part of any place else. I did not see what difference it made—certainly to us in Hill Grande—but it obviously mattered to others. Equally obviously, the meeting had had a serious mien that night.

I had little opportunity to talk with Brentwood. He seemed very much in demand as his journeyings took him over the country and he was ever the bearer of tidings, whether good or bad.

He came to our camp during the afternoon and, greeting us in his usual buoyant manner, said, "Wonder if we should not have a school class every afternoon for these members of our Hill Grande group and anyone else who would like to join in?"

"That would be up to the preachers, I'd think," replied Grandma, stiffly. "It might suit. They could teach some Bible, too."

I felt the embarrassment I always had before Grandma and Brentwood, so I did not comment.

"Well, Queen Mab," he laughed, "round up the herd as best you can. I'll go talk to the parson."

" 'Twill at least give him something to do to earn his bread and keep," was Grandma's remark as he left. Bratton barriers would have to be broken down if ever Brentwood Haynes really became my true lover, I thought.

Sophie and I had many whispered conversations about her troubles.

"Sophie, how did you intend getting married?"

"Oh," she replied, "we were going to find a preacher on the way, or an officer of the law. I would not have wanted a marriage other than a religious one but some people do have a peace officer perform the ceremony, then have it completed when they can have a preacher."

"Mmp." I considered that. "Couldn't it be said, then, that you had not had the opportunity to be married by a preacher and that now you would like to have that kind of ceremony while there is one at hand?"

"But would that not be acting a lie?"

"Perhaps acting, but for a good cause. And we surely would not say a lie. If it comes to that, we would tell the truth. Would Johnnie come down here to get married?"

Sophie's face turned white. "If his father knew about this he probably would kill me," she said. "He dislikes me for too many reasons already."

"Then we would just have to get Johnnie down here without his father's knowledge—kind of slip it in with only a few of us knowing about it."

I pondered that idea. I would need Grandma's help—but how to get it? If she knew the entire story she would be too horrified to help. I, protecting Grandma! Also, I was embarrassed to go to Father, but feeling he would have to know, I decided to tell him first. I found an opportune time and told him the entire story.

I began with, "Father, I have grown up since we came down to camp meeting."

His eyes first laughed at me, but when he saw how serious I was, he caught me by the shoulders and held me tight until I began my story. He drew a sigh of relief when I mentioned Sophie Ryan, and then it occurred to me that he thought something had happened to me. It was really a good approach, although he did lose part of the story so I had to repeat it. But in the end he was in full sympathy with Sophie.

He stood silently for some moments, then told me not to say anything until the next day after the morning services, then to tell Sophie to be ready for her husband to come for her at any time—nothing more.

To say that I slept that night would be untrue. I floated sometimes in half-dreams, but never fully unconsciously. Had I known of the other things that would transpire because of my new friendship with Sophie Ryan, I would have been even more upset.

Sophie had brought one extra dress. I persuaded her to put it on the next morning and we washed the other in the spring water, shaking it until it was about dry to erase the wrinkles. None of the heavy flat irons used in our homes were brought to camp. After eating our lunch, I told her what Father had said. She wanted to know more, but I only said, "It's big things, Sophie, because my father is at the head of it. But even I do not know what."

We waited.

Father told me the story later. Grandma did not know of anything amiss until Father and the five men he had selected to go with him to Hill Grande rode into camp. It was about two o'clock that afternoon when they arrived with Johnnie Ryan in their midst. They had ridden hard to the settlement in the early morning and found Johnnie at the barn feeding his horses. Father told him that he was to come along, that his wife at the camp-meeting grounds needed him. Johnnie swore and tore about, accused them of tomfoolery and worse, and started to the house. They prevented that and saw that he had no gun on his person, but wasted no further words. Instead, two men saddled the horse they had seen him ride, and more or less assisted him upon it.

"It will be better if your family doesn't see us leave," said Father.

"I'd say it will," said Johnnie with an oath.

"Well, I really mean it. Less embarrassment for you and that little girl."

As they rode along Father talked to the boy about the standards of our settlement—that Austin, who had first settled it, would not permit any misdoings; that the fact that he and his wife were not legally married was known only to the group who were their friends, and that if he would mind his step and go with them to be married by the preacher there would be nothing further said or done about it; that anyone bringing a child into the world had to assume new obligations, the first of which was to assure the birthright of true parentage; that his wife was upset and that, as friends, they wished only to help him right something that had been left undone only because of the pioneer conditions of our country.

As Father told me about it all, I felt both excited and moved. It must have been a beautiful speech.

But Johnnie had been sullen and belligerent all the way and the men could not feel sure he would not bolt and run. The horse he rode could have taken him entirely free of his well-meaning companions. Father talked through most of the fifteen miles. If he stopped for a moment some of the other men joined in. Johnnie did not say a word.

The campgrounds could not be seen, because of dense undergrowth, until the wagon road led up to the arbor. There the men stopped. One went for the preacher, who had been told only that a wedding was to be performed.

Father wheeled his horse about and faced Johnnie.

"Well, Johnnie?"

"Why all the palaver?" exclaimed the man. "Don't you think I want to be married? I could've got away from you any time—you know that. I sure didn't like your escort service or your approach, but I love the girl!"

He strode over to where I stood with Sophie and took her in his arms. He didn't even seem to see me.

I turned and ran to our wagon to be alone for awhile and to collect myself.

It was the first wedding I had ever seen. Father and I stood up with the couple. Johnnie still looked hostile and slouched in his posture, but Sophie's little head was raised like a queen and her smile was beautiful. After the preacher had pronounced them man and wife he undertook to advise them of the trials of the frontier and life in general. Johnnie began to fidget and act restless—he had had quite a day—and suddenly he stooped from his great height, picked Sophie up in his arms, and ran with her to their horses. Soon they were galloping away toward Hill Grande.

The remaining days at the camp meeting seemed unnatural, so quiet were the routine and the program. School in the afternoons was more like a Bible class, and Brentwood retired into the background so the preacher could lead in the discussions of the scripture. The songs, after Uncle Joe had pitched the tune, were also conducted by the preacher, Brother Jones. But Brentwood's voice sounded clear and loud over the others so Brother Jones soon conceded to him the leading of the hymns. During the evening we sat before our campfires in a circle while we had our night's prayer and songs. Sometimes for a little while Brentwood and I lingered after the other folks had retired, but Grandma seldom permitted more than a moment or two for this unchaperoned companionship before she called me in under the folds of the covered wagon. We were not permitted any diversion that would not be permissible on the Sabbath. How I longed to hear the ringing tune of "The Hunter's Horn" round sung there in the deep woods and to listen for the echo as it came back to us!

All sounds are delicately attuned in the woods. The unusual noise of song and laughter of our meeting grounds would attract the attention of Indian bands and wild animals—and our campfires were an all-night signal of occupation. The fear of such dangers made for a more serious attitude in the religious fervor of the meetings.

One night the stillness was broken by the shrill call of the screech owl from the brush arbor. Men rushed out with their guns, and every woman in the wagons held a gun in readiness. Excitement made the air tense, but complete quietness prevailed.

There was a rustle of our wagon curtain, then the whisper, "Neleetah handle—no shoot."

That was all—the stealthy visit to each wagon group.

"Grandma," I whispered, "that was Neleetah. He said don't shoot, that he will handle this."

"That Indian!" exclaimed Grandma. "And he probably can."

In a little while the call of a dove was the only other unusual night sound—no shot had been fired, no arrow had whistled through the night. There was just a subtle slithering noise as figures melted into the darkness. Suddenly the old sweep which was used to call assembly sounded loud and sharp in the continued quiet. Every man jumped to his feet and, advancing, found Neleetah, the old Indian, standing near the pulpit.

"Fine," he said to his astonished white friends. "Tonkawas like religion." He gave a swift signal of farewell and faded into the darkness.

Those who did not know Neleetah could not understand, but we knew and gave him our silent prayer. Too old to keep up with his wandering tribe, Neleetah, last year, had chosen our neighborhood to settle down. His small tent, wigwam to him, would be in one spot one day or week, and later in another. But often he came to the settlement, and he never failed to come to Grandma's door, where she loaded him down with any provisions on hand. Corn and blackstrap molasses, his favorites, were ever ready for him. Meat he could provide. Blankets Grandma had given him, to our own loss. But the security she felt he gave in exchange, the friendliness he conveyed to other more belligerent tribes than even the Tonkawas, was surely good return.

He had probably been on the outskirts of our camp all during the week.

HOME SEEMED SUCH a tranquil place upon our return. How could I ever have been the innocent child who had gone to meeting ten days ago? Not that I regretted my experiences. I had simply grown up. And I had made a friend. I must go to Grandma soon and ask the questions that disturbed me. But busy days occupied my thoughts. I went down to see how Steve's mother had fared. She was well, but Steve was not at home. He had gone that morning to take their only load of cotton to Groce's Landing to sell. It would not bring much, but that and a load of corn was their year's living.

Something I recalled filled my mind with fear. Steve going over that road—and alone! I could not let his mother know of my concern, so I told her I would come over early the next morning. Mrs. Adkins was a brave woman but she was not strong. She had trouble breathing at times and she thought it must be her heart. There was no doctor to attend her, so she had just lived quietly and said she was feeling better now. We hoped she would recover in the bracing Texas air.

I wanted to see my new friend, Sophie, but decided she must make the first advances. She was newly married, after all, and in new circumstances. Also, it was some distance to their home and I had no horse. She could ride over to see us.

School would be resumed the next week. Grandma and I carded cotton and spun the thread. Weaving could come later. Uncle Joe used the new corn grinder that he and Father had made and was storing up a supply of cornmeal. Father was busy at the shop, working on a large order of gunstocks and wagon wheels. Nerves were tense, and people didn't laugh so much. Did it mean war? Was Mexico going to drive us out? Or were we going to fight to stay? I didn't want either one.

''Your redhead woke me up early this morning to make him a new linchpin for his cart,'' Father startled me by saying as I served him a late breakfast one morning. Uncle Joe was working nearby.

''Who, Steve?'' Already my heart had quickened its beat.

''Yes. When he was coming home from Groce's, after selling his cotton. His wagon wheel slid off and crushed, and he found that the linchpin was broken in two.''

''They were after the money!'' I breathed.

''What?'' asked Father.

''Nothing. Only, oh Father, can't someone find out who is doing all this on that road to the ferry? No one is safe. I was worried about Steve when I heard he had gone.''

''What else have you heard?'' asked Father.

''Nothing, actually. Just what I surmise. Mr. Roan—now this—and we don't know what else, do we? That's the trouble.''

''My child, don't get excited. These are frontier roads and there are Indians—''

''But that man that night said it was *not* Indians then. Remember? And Indians do not murder for money. They want food. Was Steve all right?''

''Sure,'' replied Father. ''He turned his oxen loose and came home through the woods a shorter way. You can't lose that boy. He'll probably be home tonight with his wagon, all safe and sound.''

''Woman's intuition,'' I heard him mutter to Uncle Joe as he arose from the table.

''Well, Andrew,'' Uncle Joe also spoke in an undertone, ''that pin was whittled nearly half in two.''

''Shush!'' whispered Father.

I found it convenient to spend the afternoon with Mrs. Adkins, taking my sampler along so it would appear that I was busy. Hours passed and the sun was sinking behind the clouds when I heard Steve's voice, calling to his oxen. He sounded cheery enough. I waited until he had greeted his mother, then asked if he were going after buttermilk, stating that it had not been ready for me to bring. As tired as he was I hated to do it to him, but I was saving his life, so why not?

He sensed there was something amiss and we started down the road.

''Steve, tell me all you know about it,'' I begged.

''About what? Oh, that. Nothing. Wagon wheel broke.''

''Now, 'truly, truly, not unduly,' '' I quoted.

''Well, I'm here safe and sound, am I not? So let's not worry over unbroken bridges.'' He smiled. ''Just a broken wheel, and I happened to have another.''

''But not another linchpin, or I trow we would not have known of the trouble. And, Steve, you still have your corn to take. And your mother must not be worried.''

''That's just it, Linda, and we can't afford to talk. She is not going to know. Will you cross your heart, Miss Mystery, since you know so much?''

''Yes, Steve.''

''When I take the corn, Neleetah is going with me—but unseen. Now let's see who can keep a secret.''

''As well as even Neleetah, Steve! Thank you. I could not bear to think of it any other way.''

6

OCTOBER IS A beautiful month in Texas. Dry September preserves the fragrance of the blue aster and the goldenrod, the misty whiteness of the mountain snow, and the tang of the grapevine. The Spanish mulberry's purple plumes add color and perfume of unique variety. When these are mingled with the pungency of the leaves as they fall, and are dampened by the morning dew, a spicy fragrance permeates the air. An early frost turns the oak leaves to yellow, orange, and brown, and the sumach to vivid yellows and reds. The groups of cedar and yupon in low shrubs add the vivid green that creates an earthly bouquet of immense expansiveness. I love the fragrance of the cedar, fired by the heat of the midday sun and loosened in the night's chill. I love to shuffle the dry leaves of the hickory nut tree with my bare feet and to seek the nut hidden there. No wonder the squirrels lay away ample supply of its goodness. The nut, too hard for the human hand to crack, is easily their feast because of the chisel teeth with which nature supplies them. During the early winter days, Grandma kept me occupied picking the meat out of the nut with her promise of molasses candy in which the goodies would be included. In winter she made the horehound candy more appetizing with hickorynut meats before she used it to doctor our sore throats.

School carried on in spasmodic sessions. Brentwood was away from the settlement about as much as he was around the schoolroom. I went by each morning. Often there were a few others, but after visiting or exchanging the latest bits of news they would disband and go about their employs. I seldom lost an opportunity to stand at the front in the instructor's place, and, with a pointer made from the slim branches of a willow tree in my hand, I liked to go through the motions of teaching school. To teach school was my steadfast ambition. And not in a small room like ours, but in a new, beautiful building with shining mirrored walls, curtains draping the glass windows—in a girls' private school.

"Now, Miss Amher, let us hear you give the first stanza of 'The Cotter's Saturday Night.' Not so fast, Miss Amher. You must learn to recite impressively."

Then I would turn to dance briefly with an imaginary partner about the small enclosure before—"Oh, I forgot, I am a school madam!"

It was all a make-believe world if I wanted to be a young girl. If I wanted to learn to be a woman, I walked the miles to Sophie's, hoping her husband would be away from home. For hours we would sit whispering as though the outside world were at the door, she answering my questions with her wider knowledge of life, then laughing at my consternation. She was very happy, and I learned to appreciate the things she told me about—told in a more softened manner than I might have received from Grandma with her stern beliefs. I wonder!

I often went to Father's shop in the mid-afternoon with a pitcher of grape juice, saffron tea, or whatever drink Grandma had on hand. One afternoon I found the shop filled with men. Father was splitting some clapboards to cover our new smokehouse. Everyone was talking.

"But Austin's too busy taking care of the Mexican Army to pay any attention to our problems. And you shore don't think we're going to let those varmints get away with that kind of business! Looks terrible suspicious, to me, now—"

"Bet anything, if we knew the murderer of Jack Roan, 'twould be the same bunch of rascals."

Other remarks filled the shop. I was so startled I stopped at the door, holding the pewter pitcher in my hands.

"Friends," Father unbent his tired back and stood up tall. "I am as much for a peaceable community as any of you, but—"

He was interrupted by a loud "Hurrah!" but he held his hand for silence.

"You have come to ask my help. I cannot consent conscientiously to help kill a man, even if he has committed a crime, until he has had an opportunity to defend himself. And we have no definite proof. This looks mighty bad, but the crime was averted, it seems, for which we thank God. But the culprit should be apprehended, and, if found committing a crime, given a trial and—"

"And permitted to do a few more murders, steal a few more loads of corn—"

I could not stand longer. I set the pitcher down on a stack of wood and ran down the road as fast as I could.

Steve's mother was lying down on her little bed and she seemed to be sleeping peacefully. I went around to the back of the place. Steve was chopping away at a large log for house wood. He heard me before I almost slid to a stop in front of him, mopped his brow, grinned, and said, "Howdy, Miss Mystery."

"Steve, what happened?"

" 'Twould be a tale to tell," he said lightly, but his mouth was grim.

"But you are all right. Did you lose the corn?"

"No, nor my hide," he mimicked, but he took me by the shoulders and looked down into my face. Steve was much taller than I. "If I don't tell you, I suppose you'd die of curiosity."

"No, Steve, not curiosity. I am anxious."

"We may not be over the anxious period yet," he said, looking out over my shoulders into the forest. "But you should not know. The less said the better. Only this for now. I was to have been trapped. Neleetah prevented that. Can't you wait for a while and hear the rest from your father?"

"Father?"

"Yes, Linda. I don't know what will be decided or what may happen. But you and I must not take part in it. Just be careful."

My eyes were wide. "All right, Steve. And will you?"

"Most shore, I will." Picking up a load of the wood he went toward the back door of the little home, thus dismissing me.

I saw the shotgun standing by the steps. Then I turned and walked swiftly toward my home. When I came near it, I ran.

7

DAYS PASSED, days made up of hours of anxiety for the people of Hill Grande. Everyone watched everyone, but no one said anything in the open. Eyes shifted without meeting. Groups of men lounged about the trading post, at the shop, at the schoolroom door. During Sunday's brief worship and prayer service, faces were somber and unsmiling. My anxiety was kindling to a flame. Surely these people were tense with worry. What was it? Father avoided the questions, formed on my lips but never uttered because of the expression on his face. Uncle Joe shuffled out as soon as supper was over and walked down to the widow Roan's. Grandma knitted with her new cotton thread. I sat on the steps listening to the twilight call of the dove, the evening serenade of the katydids. But I had told Steve I would wait.

News I did not always understand came of developments in a campaign for our independence from Mexico. Gonzales was to keep the cannon! Ben Milam was at Goliad! Austin was mustering the courage and the troops to take San Antonio! And constant whispers of personal antagonisms in various sections of the country, interfering with duty and the right to proceed, and making the concentration of any one action difficult. The country was becoming divided more and more in what should have been a common interest.

Some, like Austin, were for the enforcement of the Treaty of 1824, by which Texas would remain with the Mexican government but would have more colonial rights. These were conservatives. Others demanded independence, as there were now more Anglo-Americans in Texas than there were Mexicans, and they had, as either invited or—later—permitted colonists, done more to tame the wilderness than anyone else had. Or so they said. Victories at Gonzales, and many other small skirmishes, had increased that second group into quite a radical party. Austin pled for the conservative idea, Sam Houston was one of the growing radical party.

"No wonder," mused Grandma, "that differences crop up. People here from every state of the Union, from across the ocean and seas; some here to make homes, others for adventure. Who could leaven the ideas and actions of such a peoples?"

"Austin!" I said proudly. He was still my hero. But Grandma meant God and went down on her knees then and there and we had our evening prayer.

"God guide our hands and our hearts in this, the building of a new country. . . ."

It was about the middle of November. A slow, misty rain covered the open places and made soft music of the oak leaves. I had retired early as Grandma usually wanted her rest almost as soon as the darkness had set in.

Suddenly we heard quite a commotion down at the trading post, and Father and Uncle Joe left the house hurriedly.

"Malinda, stay indoors."

Father knew he need not say more, but it was punishment. I lay there knowing that Grandma, too, was awake, but not daring to speak. Whatever the commotion might be, it was soon quieted down and from our distance we could hear no unusual sounds—nothing to ease the suspense of my imaginative mind with assurance. I did not know when Father and Uncle Joe came home as they went directly to their room. The next morning they were up and about as early as usual. Father's face was tragic with anguish.

"You did not succeed, Son?" Grandma's remark was more fact than question.

"No, Mother." Father gave a deep sigh. "Not altogether, at least. We rescued the old man, although he probably is as guilty as the boys. It was a terrible thing." He met my pleading eyes. "Too terrible for you to hear repeated, Malinda—but you helped bring the crimes to light and so, I suppose, are entitled to know. Two men were hanged to a tree last night. I hope you will not be called upon to witness such punishment dealt out to other human beings. There is surely a better way, even in a pioneer country."

"*I* helped, Father?"

"Yes, you helped convince me that there was more to the road accidents than mere Indian attacks. I would not allow myself to believe that we had neighbors who lived by such crimes. Other settlers were not so merciful as I would like to see them." His gesture was of defeat as he left for the shop and his step was slow and of no spirit.

Steve must tell me the entire story now, I thought. As I hastened toward his home I saw him coming toward me, but then he stopped and looked out over the forest. Following his gaze, I gasped. Two ropes dangled from the limb of a large oak tree there in the edge of the woods. Steve stood at my side and told the story.

The day he had gone with his load of corn, Neleetah had followed on foot through the woods. Silently, they had proceeded. In a low thicket-bordered stretch of the winding trail which is our way to the La Bahia road, Steve slowed the team to leap out and inspect a suspicious stretch of new dirt. An arrow flew by as he bent his head. He heard screams almost immediately. He hid on the aft side of his wagon until he heard Neleetah's signal—the call of the dove. Then he tore up the crude trap, cut a trail around it, and proceeded to the ferry. Neleetah had followed as far as the La Bahia road and had met him there on his return. The arrow Neleetah showed Steve was similar to the one that had killed Mr. Roan, and was not like an Indian arrow. But when they went to the settlement council about it, the members had said that one arrow was not sufficient evidence for much of anything. A group of enraged men, incensed to the point of lynching, went to Father, declaring that only one family would ever do such a thing, but Father had held steadily to the decision of the council. After all, that was what the council was for—to make decisions.

Plans for another trip had been made and the news about it widely spread. Then, upon a like attack, the perpetrators had been hunted to their home. There, crude arrows similar to the ones already used were found, as well as Neleetah's arrow with which he had wounded one of them.

I could scarcely raise my eyes in question.

Steve nodded and dug in the sand with his rawhide whipstock.

"The Ryan brothers," he said, then drew a deep sigh.

"Poor Sophie. That poor child!"

"Yes, but Johnnie is in no way involved. He has done all he could to persuade his brothers from committing such acts. The old father, of course, will be a problem. The council never gave its consent for such a punishment, but when the men who opposed the hanging arrived, it was too late. They also insisted that the ropes be left as a constant reminder. Hideous, isn't it?"

We looked at the tree silently for a long time.

"Yes," I whispered, "and completely ruins a gorgeous tree."

Steve took me by the shoulders and turned me around so that our backs were to the tragedy.

"But in this direction is the sunrise. And see that new settlement over there? It's a new addition to Hill Grande."

Two new houses were being built at the far end of the village. We smiled at each other. Life was still good and the future was in the sunrise. But darkness of evening again brought the tragedy about our hearts. This had to happen to our little community! Could we hold our heads high again? Could we look our neighbor squarely in the eye and pass the time of day and say that what had happened was right? Father and Uncle Joe came home to our supper of cornbread and sweet milk. No word was said during the meal, but Grandma's prayer was unusually long. In my sleep, ropes dangled before my eyes and I awakened the household with my nightmare.

The next day I went down to the shop and stopped Father at his work.

"Father, please don't think I am a baby. I am a grown woman and intend acting as such. But somehow the thing yesterday kind of cut me deep. I just couldn't believe it would turn out so. And I am sorry for poor Sophie."

"Many a strong man cringes at such a sight, my child," said Father. "You need not be ashamed. Rather let such things fill us always with horror so we will fight for the better way of life. I tried to prevent what happened. But this time there were too many against us. But it proved something—even those men who could do it are determined to maintain the standards in our community that will be a pride to our heritage. To save cotton and corn, yes, but also to eliminate unworthy characters. This will at least bring about a better way of dealing with such people. Just wait and see."

He stood thoughtfully silent, flecking the chips of his planing board from his homespun trousers.

"You are a wonderful father! I am proud of you," I said, and was answered with a comradelike smile.

Stepping-stones in the revolutions of time that lead to progress in a civilization are often the tragedies that occur in its history. The step may be a forward one, or a backward one that means the loss of ground already gained.

The Ryan boys had not lived in vain. Their deaths caused the pioneers of Hill Grande to realize a great lack in their daily lives. Father had been right.

The action which made a well-meaning citizen become a member of a mob seeking violence called for a correction of the deficiency. Our community had been small and no thought of self-government had previously come up. A volunteer council had been enough—or even more than enough. The territory of our settlement was almost on the farthest borderline of the colonies that were being established, although it was in line with many others. Settlers seldom came so far to find their Texas home. But now new homes were a frequent event in our village. Our forests rang with the cheering sound of axes and saws, the call of one worker to another. Houses replaced giant trees and thickets. We were large enough to seek self-government.

Father and the few who thought with him about the unauthorized execution of the will of the mob were able to make the forward step. Plans were laid, nominations made, and an election held. The "election" was little more than appointments as there were few who had lived in Texas for a sufficient length of time and who also desired authority in such a capacity. Father persuaded others that the men who had revolted against the recent feeling for justice should also be included in the new governing body.

Father was elected mayor, or *alcalde*. He and the councilmen, or *regidores*, the sheriff, and a commissioner's court would make up the *ayuntamiento* of Hill Grande. The new governing body filled our inhabitants with a glow of pride. We felt efficient and secure.

Part Two

Growth of Discontent

8

After the capture of San Antonio by Ben Milam, there was much rejoicing over the country. Texas was free of soldiers from Mexico! It was finally beginning to seem real to me, too. Everyone relaxed and planned to have a wonderful Christmas. Little had been done to celebrate that occasion in other years—only prayers of thanksgiving and gratitude for survival had kept the spirit alive. Now, with comforts at every hand, freedom, and the ability to progress toward the development of our goal for a new life, there was the time and the will for celebration. Then came an invitation by messenger to the Brattons to visit with the Groce family at their plantation during the New Year's celebration. There would be a dinner and a ball on New Year's Eve. The Groce family was noted for its extensive and elaborate entertainments.

Father said, "Impossible."

Uncle Joe said, "Of all things, society, at last!"

Grandma, bless her, when she saw my heart in my eyes, said, "Of course we'll go. Why not one big social occasion every three years?"

I really could not fathom them, my family. Neither could I see how it might be done, especially when I looked down at my dress, my shoes.

"That, my dear," spoke Grandma, "we'll see to at once."

And never did I doubt it, although from what source, and in such a short time? Neither did I know for many days that it was only after a long conversation with my father that Grandma pulled out the small tin trunk and took from it the folds of a lovely blue dress, merino, with braid about the low neck, full skirt, and basque, not in the present mode but lovely in color.

"Malinda," she called to me from the storeroom. "This was your mother's. Your father and I have kept it for you for just such an occasion as New Year's may be, I think. You are probably too plump, but try it on and let's see if it will do."

I was much moved. Grandma thoughtfully turned and pulled out some more garments until I could contain my emotions.

The dress was snug.

"Hold your breath," said Grandma.

I did, obediently, but finally sputtered, "But I *can't* all during one evening's dancing!"

The room rang with our laughter but I had seen tears in Grandma's eyes, also.

Shoes? That was a problem. But not for long. Neleetah brought the most delicately beaded moccasins for my Christmas.

"Gift," he grunted, and it was wonderful. As the dress was rather short, the low soft shoes were perfect although perhaps not what the belle of the season would choose. Other things would not matter. Sophie came and, when I showed her my dess, wanted to try arranging my hair to suit the dress. We had quite a jolly time pulling my long braids about. She said it called for curls. My hair was soft but there surely was no curl. She showed me how to roll it up on corn husks, tying each end into a knot to hold it up. I had a difficult time sleeping the night we experimented, but I knew I would not sleep the night before going to the ball anyway. And the corn husks really worked splendidly.

I wondered what Grandma would wear, but there was always the one convenient black dress. She said it did not matter, but I persuaded her to make a soft fichu out of one of the many petticoats that belonged to my dress. It added a very lovely party touch to her costume. We saved some flour from our Christmas baking to use to take the shine from our noses.

Christmas passed with merriment. We had a tree from the woods, candles all about, and a real cake and some muscadine wine. Brentwood came and we sang until late in the evening, all of the Christmas carols we could remember. Estelle Roan and the children were there, and also Steve and his mother. I would so much have liked to ask Sophie, but I did not. Instead, Grandma and I baked some loaves of white bread and a johnnie cake and I took them over to her. There was also a little dress made with Grandma's fingers out of white cotton cloth. Sophie smiled and blinked a lot, and then we danced around the room in sheer joy for her happiness and my excitement.

I had told Brentwood of our invitation to Groce's New Year's party. He seemed very much surprised that we had accepted.

"Oh yes," I replied. "We are really related, way back. And Grandma and Mr. Groce's parents visited now and then a long time ago. Grandma wants me to have social contacts later. This should be a lovely occasion."

"Let us hope so."

His voice did not sound convincing. But I pushed away the doubts raised in my mind by his lack of enthusiasm—especially when he began to whisper poetry in my ear and caused my blushes to deepen. I found Grandma's disapproving eyes upon me, so I excused myself and passed the cake and wine obediently.

Brentwood and I no longer met down at my tree. Somehow, since the ropes hung from that other majestic replica of my oak, I could not feel lighthearted under its branches anymore. Also, the weather was cold and rainy. School was intermittent, and, although I thought love of a true nature burned in my heart, it had few opportunities to express itself. Sometimes Brentwood's arm about my waist crushed me to him as we danced. At other times his eyes looked off into space and seemed scarcely to know of the words his mouth was saying. He had never declared his actual love for me nor asked mine in return. It was only a declaration of love in general, but my heart held it unto myself alone.

The walls of our home were thick but conversations were never held in secret. I was outside near the open door, scrubbing our knives and cooking utensils with ashes to remove the smoke of much Christmas baking, when I realized that I was the subject of my grandmother's conversation inside the room. The other voice was that of Mrs. Roan.

"I will give you the eggs, milk, meal, and whatever you need, Mrs. Roan, if you will do the cooking and feed that school pedagogue when it comes my turn to do so," were Grandma's astounding words. "It is not because I'm too lazy nor too old to do the work, but even as a bear or wild animal has the right to protect her young, I claim that I have the same right, too."

"Of course, Mrs. Bratton. You know I will be glad to help in any way I can," said Estelle Roan. "I just wondered what Mr. Haynes hisself would think."

"Let him think," Grandma's voice was louder than necessary. "I hope I do not have to order him off the place. I really want to do this without the real purpose being known, don't you see, Mrs. Roan? But if it is necessary, I can surely speak my piece. He's sticking too close around Malinda and I don't like it."

"He seems like such a nice young man," sighed the widow.

"He probably is, and I hope so, but he is just not the timber we cut our standards by. Anyway, January's my turn to feed him, and if you will do it, I will see that you are repaid.''

My ears had shamelessly sought every word spoken. Why, Grandma! was all that I could think.

The people of the settlement ''took turns'' feeding the schoolteacher, which was most of his compensation. And Grandma, looking ahead, saw complications in having Brentwood Haynes share our table. I wondered how Father felt. Did I dare ask him? The time was not ripe yet. But someday I wanted to know why it always seemed necessary to boost other people's opinion of my lover in my own thoughts.

9

How we hoped for good weather for New Year's Eve! It could so easily be impossible to drive the muddy road to Groce's Plantation—or it could as easily be otherwise. The cart was ready, the oxen at hand to be yoked to the conveyance by early daylight. I slept in my corn-husk curlers, with my ordinary shoes at my bedside, ready to jump at Grandma's first call.

It turned out to be a wonderful day, although we could not tell for sure until later in the morning when we were well on our way. Uncle Joe did not go, choosing instead to stay with the widow and saying he would keep an eye on our place. Grandma, Father, and I jogged along in the ox cart, the little tin trunk holding my precious clothes and forming a seat for me in the back. I tried to make the trip less tiring by making light—even silly—comments on things to be seen along the way. Grandma gave Father's arm a nudge as though to say: "Bubbling over with excitement." Perhaps I was, but I felt these two parents of mine were making the trip for me when they both would have preferred the comforts of their home to all the luxurious entertainment before us.

Or so I thought. But once at the plantation, the immensity and grandeur of which appeared like a city to me, Grandma's eyes twinkled with enjoyment and Father mixed with groups of men with all the ease of one accustomed to their company. It was I who felt out of place. Ofttimes I had to be prompted by Grandma to acknowledge some courtesy or introduction, so enthralled was I with my surroundings. The chatter of people, the gay laughter, the many activities in progress at the same time, made me feel small and insignificant. My tongue, usually so quick on the repartee, felt thick in my mouth. My dress was both pretty and becoming but the girls who flitted all about me were gowned in silks and laces, in lighter material and color, although the night was cold. Grandma's eyes showed concern for me so I forced lighthearted remarks and even laughter from my dry throat when I could break into the conversation.

I felt more secure sitting between Grandma and Father at the long dinner table. About me were people of all ages and character and I resolved to forget my embarrassment and enjoy the unique associations. My greatest concern was the long wait for food. The table was loaded with the most appetizing arrangements of fowl and venison, salads and condiments, but many toasts and lengthy speeches prolonged the wait for the service of my greatest need. Grandma and Father touched their lips to the glasses politely and raised them during the toasts but the contents remained as full. I felt I would be forced to join in someone's "toast to the country" if an end to them were not soon forthcoming. It was. The food was delicious.

I found Brentwood down at the far end of the table in a merry group of young folk. I could hear his voice now and then above them all as he led in their merriment. I tried for some time to attract his attention so he might locate us, but I did not think that he had seen us. A large, jovial man across from me at the table evidently saw my unhappy state and began to include me in his merry jokes. I decided to give him and the good food before me my full attention.

Later, as people began to roam about the rooms, I again saw Brentwood. He was standing with a gay bevy of girls. It appeared to me that he was trying to escape and come to me but later he waved to me across the room as they left. I felt that I needed practice. I needed finesse. Twilight was falling. Soon the ball would begin. I went out into the garden back of the ballroom, and, standing in front of a low shrub, began my part as I pirouetted about on the walk.

"Oh, Mr. Jones, don't you think it is—aaahhh—*oppressive* in heeer-rre? Shall we go out on the verandah? Oh, Mr. Jones, you do say the most intriguing things! What do you think we should dooo?—Umph—H!"

I felt rather than saw the figure with which I had collided. I looked downward to find the length of some beautiful velvet pants reaching to meet the shiny boots. Looking upward, I found a smiling, kindly face and my blushes were complete. I held out my hands.

"My apologies, sir." I curtsied as I had been taught. My practicing was over suddenly and surely.

"What do *I* think? I was just watching the most beautiful mimicry of the usual young lady. That is the way it is generally done, isn't it? But you do not need to feel that you must be like that, too. Somehow"—and he held me out at arm's length and looked at me quizzically—"you do not need that barricade."

He tucked my hand in his arm and directed me toward the house.

"Let's figure this out," he continued. "This new land of ours gets some very precious jewels that cannot shine often enough to keep their glitter. But who cares for the shine? It is the soul down deep that withstands the mimicry and demands of the mob, and that is the most desirable. Now I hear the music—the ball is about to begin. I am too old, my dear, to dance with you, but let's join the others. I know the very person to lead out with you."

To my astonishment, and, of course, embarrassment, as we entered the ballroom every head turned to gaze upon us and with one voice they cheered. The orchestra began the grand march. My companion placed my hand on the arm of a young man, the name of whom remained a mystery for some time to my excited ears. I was too dazed and my eyes were on my benefactor. As we fell in line in the grand march I turned to my companion to ask in a whisper, "Tell me, who is he?"

"Oh, I thought you were old friends," said he. "That is the commander-in-chief of the new army that we hope to have—Sam Houston."

I would have fainted dead away had not my partner supported me. He led me quickly to the veranda, saying, "Don't you think it is rather stuffy in there?"

I did not have another dull moment. My companion was jolly and did not seem at all patronizing. To be sure, now and then there were dances made up entirely of the beautifully dressed young women and men, but in the ballroom and equally enjoying the affair were men and women of all ages and styles—homespun, buckskin, calico, or silk, there was no discrimination. Grandma did not think dancing was very religious, but nevertheless she and Father were among those dancing the Virginia Reel. It was truly a gala occasion.

Later, when many of the older guests were sitting about the ballroom and the space showed as the great expanse that it was, Brentwood walked across the room to where I stood with my new friends and asked me to dance with him. My heart swelled with pride but I did not dare look toward Grandma.

Thus it happened that when the bells outside rang in the New Year, Brentwood stood at my side as we joined hands in a huge circle about the room and the orchestra led in the singing of "Auld Lang Syne."

10

AS I THINK BACK NOW, I do not feel that we should have been surprised to have Uncle Joe tell us, on the evening of our return from the New Year's party, that he and the widow Roan were to be married. No one spoke. Then I hugged his neck and was about to exclaim something in my excitement when I noticed Grandma's face. I was shocked at its ashen appearance. Father arose from the table, laid his hand for a moment on Uncle Joe's shoulder, and went out without a word. Uncle Joe went over to Grandma, where she sat as though graven from stone, and said, "Well, Mother?"

"I'll talk to you later, Son. Give me time, will you?"

Later I heard her prayers from down at the outhouse Father had built for her and me. She used it quite often for her "lonely prayers," as I called them when she did not pray with some of us. From where I huddled near the doorstep it sounded so much like groans I was frantic. Uncle Joe had been standing under a tree in the yard for some time. I went to him and tucked my hand in his pocket with his hand. We grasped fingers there. After a while he pulled my hand away with his and, patting it with trembling fingers, dropped mine and walked hurriedly into the night.

Of course there was no use in protesting. It was just that Uncle Joe was her baby boy, and also, perhaps, it was the memory of my mother's tragically short life. But Grandmother's face was soft and serene when she came into the house.

"Malinda, it has been a big day. Let's get to bed."

"Yes, Grandma." But I wanted to hug her lonely heart to mine. There seemed to be no earthly person to help Grandma fight her battles.

"Finding the right man is hard enough," said the widow Roan teasingly one evening as we sat around our front door talking of the wedding. "But getting a preacher to do the ceremony is still harder. We can't set the date until we know when a preacher can come to marry us."

"I'll just have to take a day or two and ride over to La Grange and see when Brother Jones can come over," said Uncle Joe.

The triumphant glance that Estelle Roan sent toward Grandmother seemed to indicate that she felt success assured in her method of placing Uncle Joe at the head of her house. The date was postponed but plans for the wedding were under way.

The settlement of Hill Grande, being, as it was, on the outer fringe of the colonies, was becoming the center of many exciting groups—newsbearers of the fighting between the colonists and the Mexican soldiers. After the consultation between the conservatives and the radicals was called in November, at San Felipe, and most of the representatives agreed that we should be a state within Mexico, they elected Henry Smith of Columbia as president. But there seemed to be no centralized power for action on important issues. Victories at Gonzales, Goliad, and Mission Conception at San Antonio, however, increased the confidence and determination of the colonists and led not only to the notion of independence but created an idea of invading Mexico itself at Matamoros. This plan was opposed by General Houston, but the officers of the various armies failed to cooperate with their chief. Too often decisions were left to the popular vote of the men of their army and there was no power to enforce orders.

Hill Grande residents, discussing these actions, were loud and vehement in their protests and soon it was evident that our people were strongly in favor of independence and in sympathy with General Houston. I was deeply hurt at such lack of faith in our benefactor, Austin. He was my idol. How could one go against his wishes when he had been our father and friend, when he had suffered every known hardship for his colonists, holding his own life in danger to ensure our well-being!

But Father told me that Austin, too, had now decided that independence from Mexico was the feasible action. And when he was chosen for the great mission of representative to secure aid from the United States, my heart could still swell with pride and also join wholeheartedly in the problems and projects of my New Year's friend, Sam Houston.

I heard the conversations around the anvil in the blacksmith shop, around the creation of new carts, guns, and supplies for the soldiers. I watched the men leave to join the fighting forces; I watched for Brentwood's coming and sped him away with a prayer, but he seemed to have little time anymore for songs or story. My heart contracted with pain. I sat in the little schoolroom mornings, and on our doorstep evenings, trying to think cheerful thoughts, trying not to imagine unworthy things.

I must keep my courage, too, because women would have to fight many battles if the things discussed by the soldiers and volunteers should ever come to pass.

Uncle Joe had seen the preacher and the wedding was set for February fourteenth—Valentine's Day! Also the day after I would become seventeen years of age!

"Almost a young lady," Father often said now as he brushed my hair or cheek with a kiss. I wondered. I felt sometimes that I was a grown woman, with my womanly thoughts and duties.

One morning Grandma and I were preparing Bossy's rich cream and milk for churning. We made a wonderful cheese called "curd" or "cottage cheese" out of the milk after the cream had been skimmed off into the churn. The thick clabber was encased in a cloth bag, the ends of which were tied securely and hung in the shade of a tree down by the spring. When all of the "whey" had dripped out, the result was a delicious dish, especially with cream and syrup on it. The running brook was our cupboard for the milk. We had built a small room of rocks where the water was shallow, some of it falling over the top and dripping down like a waterfall. There the milk and butter were stored in pewter pitchers covered with dampened cloths until the rich cream came to the top.

I was churning, that morning, when I heard my name called, and on going to the door I saw Sophie sitting on the bare back of their horse.

"Sophie! Should you be riding horseback?"

"It won't hurt, Malinda," she replied. "Anyway, I had to get help. Johnnie is having a time with his father. He's sick and is having hard chills and talking out of his head. We wondered if your grandmother would go over to see if she can do anything for him."

Grandma had come to the door and, after asking a few questions, quickly gathered her sack of medicine supplies, tied on her slat sunbonnet, and gave her directions to Sophie and me.

"Malinda, get your father to hitch the oxen to the cart and you and Sophie come on in it as soon as you can. Tell him he might come too, if he can leave. Bring that old quilt off'n your uncle's bed. The widow can soon supply him with another one. Put that black pot in the cart—may need it—Get about three cakes of the driest of that soap, a couple of those old sheets. Better bring the oldest weed broom. There may not be one handy."

Then, to my horror, Grandma led the horse to the stump of a tree, jumped upon his bare back, tied her bag of medicine to the rope halter, and dug her heels into the animal's side. Her full skirt spread over the back of the little horse. He was rather old in years of service, or I fear there would not have been much left of Grandma! When he started, the breeze whipped the skirt of his rider about like a billowing sail and he bolted down the trail.

I screamed and called after her. I did not know Grandma could ride a horse. But she gave a wrench to the halter which tightened on the horse's mouth so that he was won to submission. Sophie and I then hastened to Father and we were soon on our way, expecting to have to pick Grandma up from the dirt road somewhere along the trail.

When we reached the log and mud-daubed house, smoke was boiling from the chimney. Johnnie was carrying in loads of wood. We could hear Grandma's voice, singing and talking:

" 'And when weeee reach, thaaaat golden shore'—Mr. Ryan, now you'll just have to lie quiet and take this. It's not going to burn you any more than it's blistering my hands right now and you know you are feeling better already. 'We shaaaall no longer rooaamm'—how a human could let himself get so filthy—I ought to scrub you with ashes! No doubt those chills is just nature revolting against the dirt."

We went into the room and saw Grandma wringing out a heavy woolen blanket from a steaming bucket of water, and she and Johnnie wrapped the now nude and almost blistered body of the old man in it—not too gently—and rolled him into it like a papoose. She had found him in convulsions, and first soaked his feet in hot water and mustard. She had poured whiskey and laudanum down his throat. As he began to revive, he cursed with all of his available strength but was forced to remain submissive from sheer weakness. Johnnie was frantic with anxiety. But as he and Grandma continued to work with the patient, she marshaled the others of us to duties in cleaning up the place.

Evidently nothing had ever been thrown away or burned. Liquor bottles, cans, leather hides that had not been properly dressed, and old clothing lay all about the room. The two bunks where the brothers possibly had slept were banked with the accumulation of months—a saddle, guns, some of their clothing, and even sticks of wood for the fireplace. Grandma ordered everything burned that Johnnie did not want. The bunks were broken, one was removed entirely, and we began to clear the other so we could move the patient to it while we cleared the clutter with which his own was loaded. We scattered ashes all about to "purify the air," Grandma said. We cleaned out the fireplace and scrubbed pots and cooking utensils clean of some of the grease and dirt.

Grandma then cooked some cornmeal into fine mush, and before we left Mr. Ryan had eaten some. He asked for whiskey and Grandma gave him some with quinine in it. He spat it out, but when she told him what it was, he asked for more and seemed grateful. He watched Grandma as though she were a wolf, or at least in that clothing.

Before we left him with Johnnie and Sophie, she gave him a long lecture. He had to take it, but his eyes snapped and he looked at Johnnie as though pleading to be spared. We then all knelt and Grandma prayed for his recovery, that he might be given strength to take his rightful place in the community, that he might be shown the righteous way of living and stop being a nuisance to his fellowman.

I could not help peeping through my fingers now and then at the fellow lying there in the bunk. He scowled at first, but later I saw that he watched Grandma with interest. She was really serious in her intent to cure and heal both body and spirit, and her earnestness was conveyed to his doubtful mind. When we told him goodbye, and Grandma said she would come back if he needed her, the old man's eyes followed her to the door. Father said he pressed his hand as though in appreciation.

It may be put down in these chronicles that this scalding of hot water and immersion in religion that Grandma brought to him caused him to forget the animosity that had made rancor of his whole soul and he was ever afterward a friend of our family. When Father said something to Grandma about it she said, "Umph. It just got the dirt off'n him enough so that some sunshine and goodwill could reach his skin."

But it seemed as the days went by that it must have been more than skin deep. And I was so grateful for Sophie's sake.

The wedding was quite an ordeal, not only for Grandma but for all of us, especially for the Roan children. In her confusion, or because she did not realize the importance of it, Estelle had not explained the occasion to them in a way that prepared them for the excitement of the day. Jim and Jane were fond of Uncle Joe but the tragedy of their family was still a sensitive spot around the word "Papa." They became nervous as preparations caused adults to push them aside in haste. Jane became irritable and began her ever-ready tears. Jim felt always in the way. In order to meet the situation and to relieve their loneliness, I told Jim to take his sister and look for violets around the spring. I had found a few and thought how lovely it would be to have some for the bride to wear. The children were otherwise forgotten in the confusion of the last minutes.

The wedding was set for eleven o'clock in the morning. There would be dinner on the lawn for all the guests at noon. Naturally, it fell our lot to provide this feast. But some friends of Uncle Joe's furnished a yearling and it was barbecued. Grandma baked chicken pie, stretching out our precious flour with johnnie cake. About an hour before the time for everyone to assemble, the tables were ready, the bride was dressed in her new blue calico, and Uncle Joe was in the store-bought suit from New Orleans. I could not wear the merino dress because of the memories it might bring, so I wore my best homespun instead. Grandma refused to dress up in the fichu and looked sad in the black dress.

I pinched her cheek gently and said, "Smile in the face of adversity. After all, you still have Father and me, and, actually, you still have Uncle Joe."

"I probably do, at that," said Grandma.

I took out a small table for the preacher to stand behind and then brought a pitcher of fern and yupon berries for the decorations. I had just thought of Grandma's Bible and wondered if she would permit the use of it when we were startled by the screams of the children. Jim came down the path from the spring, half carrying his sister. His face was chalky white and Jane's was red from weeping.

"Snakebite," said Jim, and he fell to the ground from exhaustion.

Father whipped out his knife and, leaning down, made a cut at the spot indicated by Jane, quickly sucked the blood from the wound, then spat it out, over and over. Someone poured whiskey down Jane's throat. This strangled her and caused much spitting and scuffling on her part. Estelle began to cry and wring her hands. The liquor made the child very stupid and drunk but other things finally quieted down. The rattlesnake, a small one, was found and killed.

The wedding proceeded almost on schedule. I sat on the ground and held Jane's head in my lap as I did not want to miss the ceremony. I listened carefully to see if there were any differences in this and the ceremony we had for Sophie. I wondered how long it might be before I would be saying "I do." I thought I must start to practice soon, in order to get the proper inflection for those wonderful words. Estelle said them in her clear, shrill voice, but Uncle Joe became rather embarrassed in the quietness and then said, "Well, yes, shore I do."

The preacher almost lost his place in the book. Sophie and Johnnie were there and I saw her kiss him after the ceremony.

The celebration continued until late afternoon, but, as many had come from afar, there was someone leaving all during the afternoon. Grandma offered to watch over Jane during the night and said Jim could stay with her, too. A neighborhood custom of charivaring the newly married couple would be a harrowing experience for the children, and we were glad to spare them that excitement. There were few weddings in our country and we knew the fun-makers would not overlook this opportunity to practice that bit of early pageantry.

In the midnight hours we heard them—the noise of sweeps, horns, and tin buckets, the yells as of an Indian raid, screams imitating wild animals, all of which increased in volume until the newlyweds brought out the cake and wine that would complete the celebrations of the day.

I remember I hoped that such a custom would be forgotten before I became a bride.

11

DREARY, COLD WEATHER made the short days of February seem very long. I missed the companionship of my Uncle Joe and seldom had the opportunity to carry on the bantering conversation with him that had been my delight—his endless jokes and his numerous attempts to snare me in some game or contest. Of course, his new children were now the recipients of the pleasures that had been mine during childhood. But I would never be too grown for such entertainment. Feeling that I was selfish, I joined in the amusement of the children and shared in the enjoyment, as well as tried to assist.

I still maintained my playhouse down by the spring, although I had scarcely been there since I met Brentwood. It had always, before that, been my pride and joy. But after Brentwood, it had somehow come to seem like the past to me, even a childhood, while *he* was the future. There had been something in that feeling that had seemed disloyal, although to whom or what I was not sure. But now, after our two weddings, my feelings had changed again. Maybe, after all, the playhouse was part of the future, too.

There were the remnants of the beautiful ornamental woodwork and carved decorations which were the broken parts of my mother's organ. We had started from Tennessee with the organ, the emblem of my mother's songs and lullabies. It had been disassembled in order to pack it in one of our wagons. In crossing a rocky river bed, in that journey to Texas, the little wagon was overturned and most of the contents were lost or damaged. The body of the organ remained intact but battered, but the beautiful mirrored top with its carved woodwork had fallen out on the rocks and was broken and ruined.

I had picked up one or two large pieces of the glass and cherished them all the rest of the way, and for several years the larger fragment was all the mirror our home knew. The carved frame and candleholders were in my playhouse. They are still there, with the ground moss I planted for the green plush of my "carpets" growing about them.

The organ was mended as well as my artistic Uncle Joe could manage, but it had lost the ivory from several keys and that could not be replaced. When the occasion arose during any performance to use that part of the keyboard, these keys had to be lifted to position by the organist. The interruption was always the occasion of amusement, but also embarrassment to the performer, and resulted in the necessity of selecting songs that did not require those bass notes.

The bric-a-brac in the playhouse was ever a stimulus to my pride and inspired me with visions of a home made beautiful with mirrors and carvings for some future day in Texas. I had never had anyone to share these dreams with me, but now I had Jim and Jane, and we again made my playhouse alive.

Estelle, left to her own devices, met with the other women of the settlement in sewing circles, cotton cardings, or quilting bees. Grandma attended many of these, but most often the meeting convened at our home so she would not need to face the outside cold and rain.

Dinner was served at our home at eleven o'clock in the morning as the hours from a five o'clock breakfast until noon were too long for the working man. Uncle Joe, accustomed to such hours, found that he could partake of our earlier meal, then go home and eat his family dinner with ease. Since Estelle was not a cook of any ability their meal was usually cornbread with butter or fried meat and black coffee. But Grandma continued to set out her bait for her youngest son in the most appetizing manner, smiling one of her crafty smiles when Estelle complained of "Joe's lack of appetite." But we continued to enjoy Grandma's famous cobblers with rich cream, turkey, and now and then a fried chicken. But our flour bin was getting low and the weather prohibited a trip to Groce's Landing for new supplies until later in the spring.

There was little news that might be disturbing over the Texas settlements during those early February days, but groups of men met at the shop evenings and Saturday afternoons. Father said the discussions were heated at times. Differences of opinion regarding the new government in Texas, doubts as to the entire withdrawal of the Mexican army, and the safety of the settlements were endless subjects of debate. In the meantime plows were being sharpened and tools made ready for the crop which must be planted soon.

Brentwood continued to keep the usual school hours but seldom did I see him during the weekend holidays. My furtive questions as to his whereabouts brought noncommital shakes of the head from both Father and Uncle Joe. There was much need for him elsewhere or he would be at Hill Grande. It was the not knowing that upset me.

It was the twenty-second day of February. I remember because we had talked of George Washington at breakfast and had compared him with Austin. The day had been cold and rainy, sleet fell during the night, and in the early morning the drain to the water barrel at the back door had a fringe of icicles. During the evening I was popping corn at the fireplace, hoping Father would get home to eat some while it was hot. Grandma was resting on her bed.

Steve burst in the door and stood there, pale and breathless.

"Steve, what is it?" I ran to him but he was motionless.

Grandma arose, saying, "My boy, what has happened?" Grandma always was fond of Steve.

"My mother's—gone!"

"Gone? Where?" But I felt silly as he turned from Grandma to me. "Oh, no!"

Grandma began to put on her heavy coat and I pulled a hood over my hair. We went down the trail, following Steve.

"Go by and get your father, Malinda," said Grandma.

Steve had found his mother when he came in after doing the chores. He was there to hold her hand as she quietly slipped away. She looked so peaceful, as though she were only asleep.

We stayed with Steve until Father could return to the shop. He said Johnnie Ryan had been there and we would need Johnnie. Later Sophie came to stay with us and Johnnie rode toward La Grange to find a priest. Father, and all the other men who could, gathered at the home and sat up with Steve and his dead all night. Johnnie had to ride to Goliad before he found a *padre* who could come to perform the last rites for Alice Adkins, but we waited until he came.

Father had made a beautiful casket for her. We used some soft, carded cotton and lined it with white linen from a coat we found in her things. She had never worn black but there was a dress of light blue which Steve thought might have been her wedding dress. We laid her to rest under a large oak tree down in their pasture.

All during the days and hours, Steve had not shed a tear. He seldom said a word, his face was tense, and his eyes were set.

"Grandma, shouldn't Steve cry?" I asked after the funeral, when we had gone home for the night.

"Men do not want to be seen shedding tears, my dear," said Grandma. "Steve is growing up. His heart is broken but he probably will not cry it out. It would be easier if he would."

"Oh." Steve grown into man's estate! I went over to the wall where hung my piece of mirror and looked long at the face I saw. I turned my head about and made various expressions to see the effect. I did not want to grow up without knowing how it made me appear to others. I really felt different inside.

In a few minutes, the door opened softly and Steve stood there. Grandma and I were sitting before the fire, the glow of which lighted the room. Steve almost ran to Grandma and, burying his head in her lap, sobbed as though his heart were dissolving into tears. I really felt better, although I cried, too.

I felt I would have to have a talk with Brentwood. Surely there was something troubling him and everything could be discussed frankly and difficulties smoothed away. If I had made some mistake, I would want to right it. I waited for my opportunity and one afternoon after school I lingered until everyone else had gone. Steve had not returned to school since his mother's death so I did not expect him to go home with me.

"Won't you walk down to the house, Brentwood? It has been a long time since we had a song together."

"Oh, who could turn down such an invitation from the queen of the fairies!" he bantered, much like his old self. "Grandma won't mind?"

"Oh, I don't know for sure. But we'll never know unless we try, will we?"

His face suddenly became serious.

"No, but she has something very precious that I do not want to hurt—and knowing Grandma, I feel she thinks I may do just that. You see, Mab, sometimes these elders of ours do know more than we think."

"Yes, Brentwood, I'm sure of that. But Grandma does not know how I feel toward you."

I knew it was unmaidenly but it was from the depth of my heart. Although I had been looking into his face, my eyes dropped and I turned to run from the room. He caught me and held me close, then kissed me full on the lips. Turning me about he held me by the shoulders. My hands were clenched. I was trembling.

"You see, Mab? If we could say that is all right—but is it? There are many things that say 'no.' You are too wonderful for a wandering troubadour."

Suddenly he loosened his hold on me and dropped his arms. He was looking toward the door. I turned to see Steve standing there, his eyes blazing, his body stiff. He came toward us with the step of a panther.

"*Steve!*"

I looked for Brentwood but he was gone. Of course, he could not fight with one pupil because of another pupil! Steve saw him leave, then turned to me, his posture softening slightly, but his hands still hard fists.

He came toward me. I could not move and with an effort I stifled my screams. I did not know this person. With a spring he was at my side and crushed me to him with so much force the breath left me, then he kissed me hard on the mouth. I felt his eyes on my face before I could bring myself to look at him. I shall never forget what I saw. I did not know it then, but it was to help in the days ahead.

He left me standing there and I heard rather than saw him rush down the path.

For a long time I stood with my hands covering the shame of my mouth, trying to bring my bewildered thoughts into understanding and self-condonement. Did ever a girl, or woman, have her first two kisses of love come from two such different men under such circumstances—and then find that they were farewells for many months, and for many living deaths of duration, if not forever?

I went to the house, shaking with anger at Steve for having erased the thrill of Brentwood's first kiss and for having interrupted our first expressions of love. Would I ever have such another opportunity?

Part Three

The Runaway Scrape

12

WAR IS A TERRIBLE WORD. Yet war was being etched into our consciousness during those last days of February. Echoes of the fact that Mexican general Santa Anna was nearing our border with a large army to "put down the insurrection," news of dissension in the government-making councils at San Felipe, all came to the groups of men around the shop and trading post. A meeting had been called for March 1st at Washington-on-the-Brazos, our capital, but no one could agree upon what should be done. Most of the men and boys of the colonies left their homes and families to join some army being mobilized—some at San Antonio, some at Goliad to join with the volunteers from Alabama, known as the Red Rovers. As these men left, others who had been with the army returned, saying that the news of trouble was offset with denials and unbelief. As a result there was much going and coming, much changing of the character of any fighting force. And few there were who were trained in the tactics of war.

At Hill Grande, we watched and waited, waited for copies of the *Telegraph & Texas Register*, our newspaper—waited for the courier.

I waited for Brentwood, but he did not return.

Crops were being planted because corn must be in the ground and gardens were an important part of any pioneer's food supply.

Then came news that the government that had been organized at Washington-on-the-Brazos had declared Texas' independence from Mexico! Although there had been many strong differences of opinion, this news was received with much rejoicing because it gave the colonists of Texas something definite to struggle for, a goal to reach. But such good news was followed closely by the tragic story of the fall of the Alamo, where that gallant little group of about 180 persons, led by William

Travis, James Bowie, and David Crockett, had held the Mexican army at bay for thirteen days, as a delaying action. They held it against an army of thousands—we heard 4,000—led by General Santa Anna. All knew they would probably die, but none had left. And die they did, that 180 against 4,000. The last ones died in hand-to-hand struggle, and they died for Texas.

It was a terrible shock but it sealed the decisions made for freedom. We tightened our emotions as the men tightened their belts and picked up their guns to join the new army being organized by General Houston. Women stood ready with loaded muskets to guard their homes.

Johnnie brought Sophie to our house. There could be no doubt of the genuine love of this man and woman as he took her in his arms in our hallway. There could be no doubt of the bravery of the Texas pioneer as he stood dry-eyed and wiped away her tears, then, gently placing her hand in mine, fled from the room and galloped away into the darkness. There could be no doubt of the struggles ahead, nor the courage needed to combat such partings. Father and Uncle Joe scarcely said a word, and avoided Grandma's questioning gaze. We knew that we all were thinking the same thoughts. I walked down to Steve's deserted home. The doors were barred, the oxen free in the pasture. Father found the milk cow with a new calf and drove both of them over to our small pasture to care for them. Grandma told me that Steve had gone to meet me at the schoolhouse that day to tell me goodbye. Was Brentwood's kiss also farewell?

In the meantime, spring had breathed warmth into the chill of winter. Flowers blossomed through the woods. The prairie and hillside were gorgeous with the blues, yellows, and reds of the wild flowers we called bluebonnets, daffodils, and Indian paintbrushes. Daisies, tiny anemones, and dark-eyed Susans grew by the roadside. The woods were full of violets—but also full of snakes. I was prevented from many excursions because Jane insisted upon accompanying me and I well remembered the experience of her mother's wedding day. Dogwood made white splotches in the bright green of the forests. New leaves of the oak and willow, the sumach, and the remaining gray of the unleafed trees blended with the dark green of the occasional cedar and created a symphony of beauty. No wonder the mockingbird sang his roundelay all during the night. Even if the distress of his country had been known to him, he would have done his bit in that fighting struggle for freedom to the utmost of his tiny throat.

No previous disaster had prepared us for the massacre of the 350 men of Goliad, who were with James Fannin and trying to withdraw—as they had been ordered—when Santa Anna and his army overtook them, and shot them every one. Nor had anything prepared us for the news that the panic-stricken families of Gonzales and all along the way of the advancing Mexican army were joining the retreating army of General Sam Houston. They were all hastening out of the country.

Santa Anna, flushed with victories, was threatening to wipe out all colonists throughout Texas. He had divided his army into sections to fan out over the southern portions of the newly declared country and no colony was safe against his forward march.

There was no sleep at our house on the night before Father and Uncle Joe shouldered the guns that would fight our part of the battle. They joined the last few men of our little village and faded into the blackness of the hour just before dawn. They hoped to meet with General Sam Houston at Peach Creek, or possibly San Felipe. There was yet hope for a final stand against the victorious Mexican army, and the pioneer—to the last man—added his strength to the protection of his homestead.

I spent much of that morning in the little schoolroom trying to adjust my own life to this most tragic, exciting phase. I was accustomed to hardships. Danger often had been at my side. Terror was unknown to me. But the fear and sadness that I had seen in the eyes of my loved ones had unnerved me to a point that I felt I must not disclose to my grandmother. She stood like a monument of courage as she sent her boys away with Godspeed. She was going about her daily duties as though the world were at peace. And I was responsible for the welfare of Sophie!

When I returned to the house, Grandma was putting our dinner on the table.

"Grandma, I need some of your stamina that I have known all my life. Now it will be important that I have some of it, too. Do you grow into it as you become older, or is it something you can store up and use in an emergency?"

"Both, my child." She stopped to return thanks for our meal, then, "You do have to practice it as you live, day by day. You have to feel too that you are storing up some for a rainy day. You have to pray for it every day. But, also, it isn't lessened by use, but rather is increased. Sometimes you don't even know you have such an aid until the need arises. But you'll have enough to carry you on. Your forebears have given you of it."

13

WE RECEIVED WORD of the movements of our neighbors from Neleetah. He came to our door one morning.

"Brattons go. Not safe here. Mexico come."

"No, Neleetah, you go, we stay," said my grandmother. "Our men will come home, find us gone, homes gone—we need to stay."

He shook his head. "Not good." He waved toward the east. "All Americans go that-a-way. Crowds safer—Go."

Just then Estelle came over, looking fretful. "Oh, Mrs. Bratton, I'll have to go. The Kelleys are going and the Finch family is packed. It won't be safe here. I wish Joe had not left me alone with these children like this. After all, a man's first duty is to his family—"

She broke down sobbing and did not see the look that came into Grandma's face. The sight of her weeping, and Sophie's eyes, hardened something in Grandma.

"Malinda, you can yoke those oxen to the cart while I get some things together. Step smart, Estelle, and gather up as little as you can make out on. There can be only one cart for all of your things, the children, and this child. You will just have to make the best of it."

She was already at the fireplace, putting articles in her medicine bag. Within a short time the cart was loaded with food supplies—meal, dried meat, beans, and some butter. There was a johnnie cake which we took along. Two blankets were all we could take and there was a bucket for hot water, some flint rock, and small wood and chips for an early possible fire. Grandma came out with a gun and packed it under the blankets. Estelle's face was filled with fear of the weapon, more than of the possible dangers of flight. Then there was the small bag of supplies for Sophie's emergency.

"It can happen any day now," said Grandma, "which makes this all a greater pity."

The children and Sophie were loaded in the cart. The oxen took a few last bites of the spring grass cropping about the door. Grandma called me to one side.

"My child," she said, and I thought there was a tremor in her voice. "I can't tell you what you have to face. Perhaps if Sophie's time comes, and it is sure to do so, Estelle will have the sense to pull you both through that. Otherwise, I am sure you are the one that will have to take care of not only yourself and Sophie, but the pack and passel of the others, too."

"But, Grandma—"

"Just try to take it in its stride, and keep up with the other families whatever you do. Try to stop at night. There is a doctor at Groce's Landing—if this mad scramble would only stop there I think the whole push would be better off."

"Grandma!" I almost screamed. "You're coming too!"

"And walk along in that mud, streaking off in the face of more dangers than a whole troop of Mexicans could bring? No, Malinda, I am staying here to welcome your father and uncle when they come home and to tell them in what direction you have gone. Don't change your course, unless the others do, too. If they should come, I would go to join you, of course. But someone needs to stay in this forsaken village.

"You'll be all right, my child. Remember the stamina we talked about. I give you a goodly portion now."

She laid her hands on my head and with a brief silence, which I felt was a fervent prayer, kissed me, and told the others to speed along. The ox cart was already down the road. I had not felt I would ever have to face such a decision. My heart seemed to be turned to lead, tears streamed down my cheeks.

Grandma took the scarf from around her thin shoulders and wiped them away, and turning me about, said, "That is your duty, my child. This is mine. May we both be successful."

I ran toward the cart, and when I reached the bend of the road which would take us out of sight I turned to look back at my home, and there stood Grandma, waving goodbye to us.

Neleetah came out to see us on our way.

"Oh, Neleetah, Grandma won't go! And she would have had a hard struggle in this muddy road. I know her well enough to feel she would walk every step rather than take the space needed—"

I could only point to the crowded cart.

Neleetah gave some exclamation I did not understand, then, taking my hand, pressed it against the worn skin of his jacket and said, "Grandma brave woman. Neleetah keep watch—you say, Godspeed?"

"And bless you, Neleetah." I kissed the wrinkled hand.

He disappeared into the forest and I felt very lonely thinking we would not have his protection. But it was either ours to give to Grandma or to hold for our own, and I felt she would need it more. Neleetah obviously thought so too.

I hurried to the cart to take the lead in my little caravan and felt much better. At least I could not show any lack of courage in this company which had been placed in my care. We were far behind the other families and could not afford to be alone.

14

MY COMPANIONS WERE a quiet group for some time after our journey was under way. The creak of the overloaded cart as it lumbered through mud, the rhythmic plod of the faithful oxen, now and then the call of a bird to its mate as though it, too, thought best to join the throng of humanity which sought to find safety—these beat upon our worried thoughts as drums in battle.

Estelle wept as she walked behind the cart. Sophie's face was pale but calm. I clucked to the team trying to hasten our progress—of course, to no avail. Mud caked upon the broad wheels and at times I had to stop to knock off some of it, to lighten the load. We had the advantage of following other conveyances, but as their wheels had been of various kinds and widths and the tracks left for us were cut and deep, the disadvantages were great. Our long skirts dragged in the tracks of many feet and soon were weighed down with the mud which clung to their folds. We could see none of our neighbors who had gone ahead, and the chances of overtaking them were small. We were safest along our neighborhood road.

When we reached the La Bahia way, we were in danger of meeting the advancing Mexican armies. This road we would travel during the night, which made many dangers possible. I discussed with Estelle the possibility of following a trail through the forest but she was unwilling to try such a venture.

"I am more afraid of Indians than I am of any Mexican army," was her decision. When I found the swollen streams long the way, I was relieved that we had not changed our course. We were able to ford those during daylight hours but the darkness would add to the difficulties. Only to reach the ferry! I felt if we succeeded in that, we might attempt anything that came farther on.

Our peace from the children's section was short. Soon Jane demanded a drink of water. That was one thing we had forgotten to provide since it seemed so plentiful all about us. There was nothing to do but stop, and take the time to lead the children down to the creek that ran its course near the road, and water them.

The routine of watering and feeding the children caused many stops and placed us farther and farther behind our companions. The children also cried continuously and fought with each other, crawling over the contents of the cart. Sophie was very pale but managed a smile when I asked how she fared. I realized that my shoes were coming to pieces and, thinking there might be more need for them later, removed them and threw them into the cart. The cool mud, oozing between my tired toes, was soothing and progress was less tiresome. Often the oxen stopped dead still and we had a moment's fear that they would refuse to continue, but encouragement in words and the flick of the willow whip sent them on the way again.

Jane became ill and had to have attention. I felt it was caused by her continuous weeping, but I could not blame the child for being upset. Jim slept from pure exhaustion, and was the more fortunate in being able to do so. I left them to Estelle, and deserted Sophie to her own thoughts, while I bent my entire efforts to our progress.

Darkness came. We were on the road alone. Later I heard a noise behind us and realized that we would have to give way to someone in the narrow road. I struggled with my team and finally gave half of the space, fearing that the effort of getting back into the deep ruts would cost us the last efforts and strength of faithful Dan and Ran, as Father called the oxen. A wagon came upon us. I was delighted to find that it was loaded with Texans, each carrying a gun. When we called to them, they answered us in good fashion and stopped to see how we were faring. They were on their way to meet General Houston.

"Someone's got to give that gen'rul enough courage to stop and fight," one man said with a curse, but with an earnestness that rang true. "He's just skippin' the country."

"Ah, now, Jed," another voice joined in. "How in the world would you know what he's up to? That general's a crafty fox. He's prob'ly layin' a trap for Santa Anna right now. Let's git going, though. He needs us."

"How much farther is it to Groce's?" I asked.

"Nigh onto ten mile yet, lady, but there's them that ain't fur ahead of you. And you'd better keep goin'. 'S'no tellin' whut devils may travel this road during the night."

Ten miles was nearer than I had feared, and, although the children awakened and Jane began to cry, we were grateful for the passing guests.

When I finally guided the tired beasts along the crowded streets of Groce's Landing, it was three o'clock in the morning. Estelle had climbed into the cart a few miles down the way, declaring herself unable to walk any longer. The group slept in grotesque positions, leaning against one another in the cart. I left them under a large tree, which I hoped would act as a guiding post for me later, unyoked the oxen, and began to search for the ferry.

There were many tents, which I learned were permanent homes. About and among these milled a mass of people—soldiers, other men, women, and children. All were too busy with their own problems to notice the tired, bedraggled figure of a girl who plucked at their coat sleeves and asked for information.

I finally got the attention of a woman. She looked at my mud-fringed skirt and tired face and said, "Well, I'm glad to see another one has made it!"

"Do you think this is far enough?" I asked anxiously.

"Far enough for what? Oh, you poor child, no. The army is crossing, they say. General Houston is going clean out of the country. And no man or woman with sense will be staying behind that army."

She hastened on her way. I wandered about and soon found that I was near the ferry. A man was standing at the boat landing, directing the loading of the ferry for its next deposit of refugees across the waters of the Brazos.

"Sir, where are we supposed to go from here?"

"Beggin' your pardon, lady, but who do you mean by 'we'?"

"Everyone, sir. I want to follow the crowd. I have two women and two children with me."

"We're loading the families as fast as we can," he said, "but may have to stop at any time to get the army across. We're waiting for orders for that from the general."

"Then, is there a doctor nearby?"

He looked at me with increased interest and I continued. "One of the ladies with me is expectin'. A child," I explained. "Any hour."

"God in Heaven!" I appreciated his prayer. "Where are your people?"

"We've just arrived, sir. I—I am not sure, but they are right around that way," I pointed, "under some oak tree. They are all asleep and I thought it might be well to wait till morning to cross."

"Young lady, you'd better get over here and start moving. I'll ask about a doctor, but there's liable to be a battle here by morning. Bring them around and I'll get you across."

I tried to turn, but instead felt myself sinking to the ground.

I revived to find burning liquid being poured down my throat. Sputtering and coughing, I opened my eyes to find several men kneeling about me.

"Well, if it isn't Alice Blue Gown," said a familiar voice. I recognized my partner of the dance of New Year's Eve. "The world is a small place."

"Oh, Mr. Crain!" My voice reflected my great joy and relief.

" 'Captain,' now, by your leave, Alice," he said. I remembered that during the evening's dancing he had insisted upon calling me "Alice." And now he was a captain!

Having the benefit of his help made the night more reassuring for me and sent me on the way with more courage. Our army was backing us. General Houston might be running from the dangers of our land, but if he were, it was best that we all do so, and I and my little group surely would follow.

Captain Crain told me of the criticism and the dissension among the soldiers, of their constant bickering and fighting among themselves.

"But we'll turn back on the vipers yet," he said.

When I asked whom he meant, he replied, "Why, the Mexicans. Let them think they are winning. Texas will win yet, say I. What do you think?"

He looked as though he really wanted to know, so with the renewed courage his kindness and words had given me, I told him of Grandma's philosophy of stamina and said that I felt that we would be given the power to retaliate when the right time came.

"Bless you, Alice of the Blue Gown," he exclaimed, and he seemed encouraged, too. "Some soldier came through earlier tonight who had been sent from the Alamo in San Antonio to escort the colonists at Washington-on-the-Brazos. They did not tarry here long. There was at least one pregnant woman in his group. I remember her, riding in a buggy. Too bad you couldn't have met up with them."

"Oh, my crippled cargo is so slow, I lost contact with even those folks from Hill Grande," I said with more lightness than I felt. "But thanks, Captain."

"Well, may your journey be a safe one, now. And here's the ferry."

It was his hands that guided our unruly, tired ox team with its wide-eyed cargo onto the crowded ferry in the confusion of bawling cattle, crying children, and cursing men.

Across the river we found a quiet corner for a brief rest.

There was no breaking of morning calm—there was only a continuation of the confusion of the night before. Estelle and I fed the chidren the best we could. We had no money but I was able to get some milk from a kindly refugee's scant supply. We rubbed the cloth of our long skirts, breaking the cakes of mud to lighten the weight of the fullness. Sophie was quiet and very pale. How I longed for a cup of hot tea for her!

Then we turned our faithful oxen down the road.

There was much confusion as to the best route to take. Many insisted that the eastern way out to Louisiana was the best, and also it was thought that General Houston would lead his retreating army in that direction. Others thought the southern road to the new capital at Harrisburg was the better plan, and that was the route already taken by many of the refugees. I wanted to go where General Houston went and scouted about to find Captain Crain, but he was not to be found. Most of the families were persistent in remaining where they were as long as the army stayed in Groce's, and it seemed that there was no movement of the main forces. Estelle thought that if the army remained there, it would be the spot sought by Santa Anna for a battle. We finally went, with the major part of the milling wagons and carts, down the winding, newly cut road toward Harrisburg.

We found many bayous to ford. These were so swollen from the recent rains that it was difficult to find a crossing that would be safe for our small cart. We assisted in carrying logs and brush to make a temporary bridge. Often two trips were necessary for one family. Once we dug down the steep bank of a stream to make a more gradual slope.

There were few men in our group. Some of the children were ill. We wondered how long the excitement and fear would boost the courage of our people. One crossing completely unnerved Sophie. The children became ill from their unusual morning's experience and Estelle began to cry in her nervousness. I sat down on a log and, silently watching them, prayed a little prayer: "Give me more stamina, Lord, if it is Thy will. I need more than my forefathers were ever called upon to provide."

But I could not afford to let my thoughts linger on Grandma for to do so sent chills of apprehension down my back. I began to sing, a song the children liked, catchy and cheerful. Jane looked at me in silence for a moment, then cried louder than ever. She seemed to think I had lost my senses. I was not sure but that I had. But no time could be lost. All of the families with whom we hoped to keep company had started across the prairie. When I flicked the senna weed switch I used to encourage Dan and Ran, they went obediently forward.

Estelle did not follow, and when I reached her to find the cause, her face was full of pain. She motioned to her foot. "It's broke, I know," she wept. "Now what will we do?"

I had to rush forward to stop the cart, then dug down into the contents to find a hunting knife.

When Estelle saw me running back to her with the knife she began to scream. What she thought I was going to do is still a mystery. I suppose it just reflected her upset state. I quickly cut strips from the bottom of my homespun dress, wound them tightly about her ankle, assisted her to the cart, and, with some difficulty, into it. By this time other families were well across the prairie, and my load, which I had hoped to lighten before we crossed that uncut sandy place, was instead made heavier. However, Jim responded to my invitation to help guide the team so he walked by my side and we began our tedious trek over the boggy sands.

Sophie had been very quiet all morning. Now I saw that she was lying back in Estelle's lap and her face was tense with suffering. Estelle answered my silent questioning with a tragic nod of her head. This, I thought, out on a bare prairie with the other people too far ahead to signal! It was late afternoon, since our crossing of several bayous had taken most of our daylight.

I decided to ignore the emergency and spend my time with the team. If Estelle had not been helpless, I might have run ahead for help. Jim was too small and there was nothing else to do. But then I had second thoughts.

"What do you think we should do, Sophie?" I came to her side.

"Just drive as fast as you can, Malinda, perhaps we'll find somewhere to stop, at least before—" and her face blanched with pain.

During the days when Sophie and I had studied her future plans we had read a doctor's book from Grandma's shelves on approaching motherhood. At the time, I had not tried to remember the various symptoms or happenings, I was merely seeking knowledge of something that had escaped me. Now I tried to recall these things and wished fervently that I had memorized them all. At least I knew that we needed help soon and a place of some protection from the rain which now and then descended upon us, a place for the convenient use of the items Grandma had placed in the little bag.

I could only hope and pray. The children were asleep. My feet, torn and bleeding, were salved only by the clay of many miles. My shortened skirt had been some relief. We needed food—at the least we needed water.

A wooded section provided water which was as clear as the mudstained hands that dipped it from the stream. The oxen drank their fill and wanted to lie down. But I prodded them until they went on, across the water, up the bank beyond, and out over another stumpy road. Some wagons ahead appeared to be waiting for us but, when I waved and called, they evidently thought everything was all right and went on their way.

Night was drawing down upon us and all that was in sight was wooded hills and bayou jungles. Surely there would be some habitation before long! Just as the night became inky black and the fireflies came out to light our weary journey, I saw a dark splotch ahead on the side of a hill. Estelle saw it and gave an exclamation of relief.

''Sophie,'' I called. ''How is that for a manger? Cheer up, all, we shall have a home for the night.''

It was not much of a home. It looked lonely and forsaken. The owners evidently had left it to seek a safer place, but to us it meant a haven in a time of great need. There was a fireplace and some dry wood, and the kitchen had some food. The beds were unmade and dishes on the table held the remnants of a breakfast.

I brought my charges in, one at a time, after I had gone over the place with the gun in my hands. What I would have done if something had appeared, I do not know. I had learned to shoot, but weariness was overcoming my ambitions for protection.

Sophie was put into the bed after we straightened up a bit, but soon she was up walking the floor. Estelle's foot pained her and she refused to see about the children. I could not afford to lose our oxen, so I had to care for them. I found a pen in the back that would hold them, with even some corn in the crib. I hung our wet blankets over the shuttered windows to prevent the glow from our fire from being seen and struck my flint to start a blaze. Hot water would be needed for Estelle's foot and for Sophie. I found some meal and started a gruel for the children, but before it was heated through they were both asleep, mudstained tears running down the channels of many others shed during the hours of travel.

The night dragged by. Sometimes I walked the floor with Sophie, sometimes she wrung her hands in pain and threw herself down on the bed. I thought I had never seen such suffering. Lack of food and rest, together with anxious hours during such trying days, surely contributed to the ordinary pains of motherhood. Often I wondered if she could live through the ordeal, as Estelle and I worked all during the night.

When the great moment came, I gave a cry of joy and turned to see

Estelle go over in a faint. A baby's cry rang out. When Sophie's eyes opened, I could scarcely whisper:

"Sophie, what did you and Johnnie name your son?"

"John Andrew," she said, and slept in her weariness.

Andrew is my father's name.

15

I HAD AGREED WITH Grandma that if we stopped on the way, I would tie to a bush on the nearest road a piece of the scarf that I wore about my neck. It had been difficult at times during the journey to hold to the scarf, but it was to be our flag for rescue and had to be retained. I went down the next morning and secured this sign of the birth of John Andrew Ryan to a clump of yupon bushes.

The road we had followed must have been an unfrequented one, however, and I wondered if it would be used by anyone else, and if my scarf would ever be seen. Yet, although here in the forest we might be found by Indian or wild beast, I felt we were safe enough from any Mexican enemy. Surely it had been a God-sent haven for us in our need, and here we would have to stay for awhile. But there remained one fear: However would we learn what had happened to the outside world, and when would we know if it were safe to return home? It depended on Johnnie Ryan.

We lived from day to day only. Sophie remained very weakened. Estelle's foot responded to hot water and, although she seemed reluctant to admit it was not broken, we decided it was only a case of strained muscles. We washed our clothes one at a time so that some of us would be dressed for any emergency. Our food would last only a few days. The baby cried a great deal as if to demand the reason for bringing him into such an uncomfortable world. We tried juice from the gruel we cooked for ourselves as additional baby food but it did not seem to suffice. We did not dare go far from our door and it was hard to keep the children happy within the four walls. I think the oxen were the most content of us all. I only hoped they would not reveal our hideout.

One morning we heard the noise of vehicles coming up our hill.

Everyone ran to the door, but we were hastily pushed back by Estelle.

"Fools, it may be the Mexican army!"

And well it might have been. Jane began to scream and before her mother could slap her hand over her mouth the sound had carried down to the road. The wagon stopped and a man and woman peered out from under the rude covering which protected them from a hard downpour of rain. The man halted and we saw they were Americans, so Estelle hobbled down toward them.

"Friends?" she called.

"Wal, yeah, Texans, if thut's what you mean," said the man, jumping over the wheel. "Whut you folks doing here?"

Judging from her gestures, Estelle told them graphically our situation.

The man and woman came up to the door.

"Thar's several more wagins coming," the man said. "We left Groce's and went toward Nacogdoches but learned the Indians were eatin' up all the folks going that direction, so we turned down this way," was his explanation.

"General Houston finally made up his mind and went toward Harrisburg," added the woman.

That was the first good news I had had. They did not know much else as they had been traveling day and night to overtake the other families. One woman of their group had been stricken and had died and was buried on the route. They had had much sickness, and the rain and high waters of the bayous evidently had increased as the days went by.

"Malinda, we must follow with these people. We don't know yet what that Mexican army is going to do, or who will win a battle," said Estelle.

I looked at her in horror and motioned to the ill Sophie and the crying baby. "But, Estelle, to move now is impossible."

"Impossible or no, I'm going," said she and began to gather up her things. "If you think more of that woman and her baby than you do of your own blood and kin, I'll just go and take care of my own."

"You'll have to go, Linda, dear," said Sophie. "I'll manage somehow. Why, many pioneer mothers have had to do as much."

"Their conditions might be different, too."

I was most angry with Estelle. "Very well, Estelle, I'll yoke up the oxen and you can take the cart. Just send some one of your friends after Sophie and the baby and me when it is time to go back home."

"Huh, you think there'll be a home to go back to, yet, don't you? You and your grandma's faith! Not me. I'm on my way to Louisiana and you can tell Joe Bratton he can follow if he wants to."

I went to get the cart in order and gave both Dan and Ran a hug around the neck. They had been faithful. I hoped they might be taken care of on the remainder of the march to freedom.

I stood in the door and waved to Jim and Jane as our cart joined in the caravan. Estelle would be safe enough and might be able to wheedle the people with whom she was going into caring for her and her children. I hoped so. But so far as I knew, she could not even yoke a pair of oxen to a cart. I turned back to Sophie and John Andrew.

"Well," I spread out my arms. "The place seems to be ours—until the owner returns, of course."

"Linda, you can never be told enough how much you have done for us. Johnnie will have to repay you. I can never—" Tears were in her eyes.

"Well, we'll just leave that to John Andrew here," I said jokingly, and chucked the sleeping boy under a double chin. I realized that at last he seemed content with his food.

16

TIME MARCHED BY. I counted the days and marked them down on the door-facing. I wondered when we might hear from our loved ones. Would Santa Anna win? Would we be forced to hide out until we could escape or Johnnie could find us? Would Johnnie be killed? I tried to think of my own loved ones, but it was painful. It was better not to try. Better to spend my thought contriving ways to provide food, to secure our safety.

I had given Estelle generously of the food we had brought, leaving only our proportionately small share. Without milk Sophie and the baby suffered. I should find a cow somewhere about the countryside. I made short excursions in the woods. I found berries ripening and stoned a rabbit to death. But I could not locate a cow. I robbed a bird's nest for badly needed eggs and prayed for forgiveness.

One day the early morning hour was broken by a welcome sound. It was so familiar to my ears that at first the significance did not come to me. It was the homecoming moo of a cow. At the back rail fence, near the little pen surrounding the small log crib, stood a cow, proudly licking the slick back of a calf. She had probably hidden out in her own way for the same event which had caused our occupancy of her master's house and now felt it safe to bring her offspring from its hideout. Somehow a cow makes living in a home more complete. I wondered if we could accept her coming as a good omen for us all.

That was the night I dreamed of my family. Father and Uncle Joe were returning and I was going down the trail to meet them. I awakened myself and Sophie by crying, "Father, are you all right?"

I could not conjecture what might have happened to Grandma. Some of the stories I had heard from the refugees along the way had filled my mind with dread and foreboding. I had no doubt of her courage. But what is courage when one is alone day after day and does not know how to prepare for the things that might happen? Her ingenuity had been evident all during the years. I had only to recall the affair of ridding the bear with a bait of honey; or the time I found her rescuing a rabbit that had been charmed by a rattlesnake; or the many occasions when, as a little child, I watched her overcome apparently insurmountable difficulties. I hoped to know before long that her decision to remain at home was as wise as were her usual ideas.

I went down to the roadside each day to be sure our flag still waved. It was getting faded and bedraggled. I washed it and shook it out so it would not be in such a sad condition.

Johnnie's "hallo" came to our sleepy ears one morning before daybreak. We always slept fully dressed, changing our clothes during the day to wash and dry them. Sophie and I met at the door head-on. But I let Sophie open the bars as we realized who was coming. I went out to tell our cow and calf that we would not be needing them much longer.

Johnnie's face was radiant as he sat with one arm about Sophie, one chucking his baby under the chin. By now John Andrew was able to respond to greetings with a broad smile. Over our milk and flapjacks, we listened to Johnnie's story—San Jacinto and its victories, the ringing battle cries of "Remember the Alamo! Remember Goliad!," Texas' freedom, Santa Anna's capture—Johnnie said that Father and Uncle Joe were at home, but his face clouded as he told us that Uncle Joe had contracted malaria and had been very ill. Father had carried him home from Groce's Ferry. Father had also had a flesh wound in his side. Johnnie had not been injured.

Grandma? She was full of experiences but had kept the thieves from her door. He laughed and said it would be more effective if I waited to hear her experiences from her. But the results of the ravages and robberies which were the aftermath of the flight of Hill Grande's inhabitants were evident.

"Just be prepared for your grandma's version of 'I told you so'," he laughed. "She is well satisfied that she did the right thing."

"And I am sure of it," I said, shivering when I remembered our experiences.

Johnnie said no word had come to them regarding our safety. He had followed road after road out of Groce's until he saw my flag. He might have missed it had not the bright moonlight revealed it to him. No news had come to them of Estelle and the children, but many refugees were yet missing from their homes.

At noon we said goodbye to our refuge and began our return to Hill Grande.

We spent the night at Groce's Ferry, but instead of sleeping on cold ground with wet blankets we stayed at the hostelry, with all the comforts of home. We retired early, but I was awakened during the night by some late arrival who seemed to create much excitement and confusion.

Perhaps the quietness of our recent retreat had made me unusually sensitive to sounds. The voices seemed familiar and the walls were thin. The sound was a disturbing element for some time. I went to sleep but later awoke with a start. The voice—it was Brentwood's! The other was that of a woman and the accent was surely Spanish. I was so upset I could not sleep longer even in my comfortable bed.

I arose early, dressed with all the care my soiled, worn clothing and ragged hair would permit, and went outside. I walked up and down the veranda of the hotel. Then I found a chair and sat and waited.

It seemed an interminable time. Everyone was up and about when I finally saw Brentwood open the door and come outside. He was dressed in a tailor-made suit of clothes such as I had seen very seldom and his appearance was immaculate. Regardless of my unkempt appearance, I arose and ran to him.

"Brentwood!"

He did not turn immediately but stopped in his forward movement and, when he looked toward me, there was a scowl on his face.

"Mab!" he cried gaily. "Fancy your being here!"

"And you?" I laughed nervously, remembering last night.

"Why yes, on my way to Shreveport. Where are you to go?"

I thought he seemed interested and began to recover from my embarrassment. I told him in as few words as possible what had been our experience. "Which," I ended apologetically, "I hope explains my appearance."

"What a tragic thing to happen to you." He was very sympathetic. "I came through Hill Grande the other day and found the place in shambles. I wondered if any of you escaped. You surely are not going back there?"

"Oh, yes, certainly! In fact, Grandmother never left home. Father and Uncle Joe are there now. I can hardly wait, of course, to see them. Santa Anna was defeated, you know, and Texas is now free and we are independent. Isn't that wonderful?"

"Yes, yes, it is." He did not seem enthusiastic. "But I am leaving Texas, Mab. On my way to Shreveport now. I had made my plans before the battle the other day but feel it is safer to go now. You see—''

''Brentwood, daaaarling, where are you?'' came the musical voice from the hallway. It was that of the woman I had heard the night before. The door opened to reveal a beautiful woman, her olive skin setting off the glory of hair black and shining in its perfection. Her dress was of white from head to foot with scarlet splotches about her in a scarf, parasol, and the plume on her sweeping hat.

''Oh, forgeeve me?'' She smiled in question as she saw me and beheld my confusion.

''Therese, this is a friend of mine, Malinda Bratton. Malinda, Therese.''

''Hees what you call, *wife*, he means,'' smiled Therese.

I felt faint. Brentwood was evidently embarrassed, and although it felt as if my heart had stopped giving me any assistance whatever, I covered my confusion as best I could and said politely, and with my best curtsy, ''I am glad to know your name, Therese,'' and then waited for further explanation.

Evidently there was none forthcoming, and Therese placed her hands on her husband's arm and, nodding her farewell to me, said, ''We promenade on the piazza only, eh, dear Breenntwoood?''

I felt my body growing cold, and my hands were damp from nervous sweat. Looking about me for some place of seclusion, I saw none and felt trapped. I could not go back into the room which had only a screen between my bed and Sophie's family. The streets were furrows of mud. Our cart was at the barn. I found the dining room and, sitting in the farthest corner, hoped Brentwood and his new wife would not decide to eat an early breakfast. I asked for food, everything I had hungered for during the past days. When it came the sight of it nauseated me. I sat and toyed with it until Sophie and Johnnie joined me. Their joy in being together made my silence appear as politeness, for which I was grateful.

Later I saw a carriage with bright leather cushions and glittering trimmings, drawn by white horses and in the control of a Mexican in livery. Then came the only two people who would fit such trappings—Brentwood and Therese. When they had gaily seated themselves, Brentwood carefully spreading the robe over Therese's lap, they drove down through the mud of Groce's streets and out of sight.

I heard their merry laughter, their chatter in pure Spanish, I watched the carriage until it disappeared, then fled into my little room. Remembering not to disturb the sleeping child, I stood with tightly clenched fists and let sobs roll out of my heart and tears down my cheeks as I tried to harden my feelings against any such hurt again, forever.

Part Four

The Rebuilding

17

I WAS PROUD TO BE a Texan, as we rounded the curve and came into view of Hill Grande. True, many of the homes were destroyed, burned to the ground or damaged by the ruthlessness of the pillagers and thieves. The trading post was looted and razed, the school building was burned. Father's shop was partly destroyed.

But Father was coming down the road to meet us. I jumped out of the cart and ran to him. He was pale and carried his arm in a sling, although the wound he received was in his side. I hugged his neck with two good arms as his left encircled me. We were too overcome for comment.

As we walked down the sandy path, my worn shoes seeping the drying sand between their soles, my dress a torn fringe about the hem, I was the picture of a returned refugee—but I was home and I was happy.

Grandma was very tired and thin. She had been nursing Uncle Joe since his return. I felt I must try to shield her for the rest of her life.

"You brave Trojan!" was my greeting.

"You true Texan," was hers.

From his bed, Uncle Joe smiled a wan welcome that so clearly reflected his lack of his usual spirit that tears came into my eyes and I could only pat the cover which was his shoulder. Everyone insisted that I tell my story. But first we fed the Ryans and saw them on their way. Johnnie had found their home well intact, as it was far from any known route. His father, like Grandma, had weathered the threats and had been able to watch the place. Their cattle were gone, as was the horse which had been the brothers'.

Later I told the story of our journey, the days and nights of the "runaway scrape," as people were calling it, making the story light as to Estelle and the children for Uncle Joe's sake. I felt we surely must hear from them soon.

Grandma said, "Umph!" But later, when I had heard some of the misfortunes of the families who had gone farther, by way of Liberty and the Colorado River, I knew that she, too, was shielding Uncle Joe.

I wanted to hear some of Grandma's story, and as Father and Uncle Joe had gone over and over it with her, we talked quietly out in the evening's moonlight as Uncle Joe slept.

Neleetah had come immediately to Grandma and had tried to persuade her to join us, failing which he assured her that he would be around and would keep watch. Grandma had warned him that she was going to bury some of the plowshares from Father's shop about the place, and to be careful how he tread. These, with the blades uncovered, did prove a weapon for creeping feet, and she laughed with glee as she recalled hearing many curses and screams when the sharp edges cut through into the feet of the thieves. She had barred all windows of Uncle Joe's home, the shop, and our house, taking her stand at an opening in one blind where she had cut a peephole. There, day and night, had been her post. At intervals she had fallen asleep.

Several times Neleetah's signal—the call of the dove, followed by the shrill mimic of the screech owl, had warned her, and she had shot through her peephole at any figures she could see prowling around. Whether she ever hit anyone she would not know, but the sound of an unexpected gun filled the night with terror for the intruders. Fires were started, and these she could not control. Many nights she went through this program.

Homes were destroyed and plundered until there was little left to encourage more robberies. Even then she had to remain in seclusion for fear of possible Mexican raids. But she lived fairly well and was worn out only from loss of sleep which she had not yet been able to recover.

Bossy and Steve's calf had been hidden down in the creek bottom by Neleetah and were about the only cattle that survived.

"When I saw Andy and Joe coming down the road," she closed her story, "I knew we had won the victory and that all was well."

Father told me later that Uncle Joe had insisted upon walking those last yards to the house so the shock of seeing him would not be so great, and that Grandma had come down the trail to meet them, shouting and praising God. Tears welled in my eyes. How grateful we always would be for the wonderful victory at San Jacinto! And how thankful I always would be to Neleetah for his faithful watching.

"Is Neleetah all right, Grandma?"

"Well, you know that Indian. I have not seen him since he came to the door the day you left, only heard his signals. We probably won't see him until some trouble arises, or when molasses is made in the summer."

Father's story was longer and certainly more exciting. I felt he was telling it in a sketchy manner, too, leaving out many hardships. He was in Groce's settlement probably the day we left there, as the army assembled during the days while General Houston waited to make his decision. Father and Uncle Joe had joined the others at San Felipe. They did not enter into the discussions regarding the tactics of the new general, but heard enough to know that plans were vague, courage wan, and feelings against withdrawal high. The Texans were whipped to the point of revolting and going to meet the Mexicans on their own. Instead of feeling discouraged by the massacres of their men, they were heated to high fighting tension. They must have revenge.

The days at Groce's were terrible ones. And General Houston was not to be found.

"I felt he was having a pretty hard fight of his own," said Father, "trying to decide what to do. It is not an easy job for even a great man to have the fate of a people and a nation on his back. Later we learned that he was in conference. The day we were told to march we did not know where, but when we turned right instead of going forward, a loud cheer went up into the heavens. The soldiers, the pioneers, the boys and the old men, knew we were on our way to battle, and the feeling was good."

The march to Harrisburg, the news that the Mexicans had been located, Father sketched only hurriedly. Of the battle at San Jacinto, the story has been told over and over as one of the greatest of the ages. Father had noticed that Uncle Joe was panting as he marched, and he saw the high color of his cheeks and knew that the going was too hard for his weaker constitution. But accustomed as he was to following his older brother in every detail, Uncle Joe plodded on and was nearby when the bullet went through Father's right side, just below his arm pit. Had he not had his arm raised to fire his gun, the bone would have been shattered. It was really a minor wound, and so high was the excitement that no attention was given to such small details and it had run into more seriousness because of neglect and exposure.

After the final arrangements for the volunteers to return to their homes, Father and Uncle Joe realized that they, with many other pioneers, were many miles from home and without transportation. Uncle Joe's fever was now very evident. Father managed for some quinine and they made their way to Harrisburg where the other sick had been hospitalized. Later, they found friends going to Groce's Landing and had come from that point slowly and by foot, with—for most of the time—Uncle Joe riding piggyback on Father.

No wonder war made brave men and women out of people who were already tempered and steeled by the affairs of pioneer life! No wonder we faced the future with assurance and faith. But we would need all of this in the days ahead.

For some time after I arrived home, I slept all day and relieved Grandma's watch at Uncle Joe's bedside at night. I think I really slept all night except at intervals when a movement from Grandma's bed awakened me in time to give him his medicine. But his fever was whipped and it was only his weakness that we had to combat. Grandma made "pot likker" from the pokeberry greens which were full of iron. Father fished down at our stream and brought in some wonderful perch. He could not use his right arm for much hunting, but he did bring home squirrel, quail, and a turkey. Grandma cared for his wound and he was recovering from the complications that had set in when he strained it in his travels and in carrying Uncle Joe. How he lived through that trek is yet a mystery to me.

The colonists were returning. Each day more axes resounded through the forest as they felled trees to rebuild homes. The trading post was soon opened and goods came in from the ferry. Johnnie and I had brought home a barrel of flour which was divided between our families and proved to be a lifesaver, as our corn was low. That which had been planted in our small farm was overgrown with weeds. Father made some some headway, however, in pulling out the overgrowth by hand while he regained the use of his right arm. The rains were less frequent and the sun added its glory to the beauty of a new land.

Grandma noticed my lack of outdoor exercise and changed my program so I might wander about the settlement in the early morning. I watched the new homes grow in each hour's labor. The schoolroom was still a pile of ashes. What memories it brought back to me! But as far as emotion, I felt there was nothing but a leaden mass in my breast. Yet I thought it was a pity, and wondered if no one had realized the need for a school. Maybe that would come later.

I went down to Steve's home. There was nothing but a shell of a house and weeds had grown up to the height of the door. I had not thought of him often during the full days that had gone by since we left Hill Grande. Where could he be? What might have happened to him? I asked Grandma and she said no one had heard from Steve, and we wondered how we would ever know where he was.

I had to stop thinking of all that, and began to reestablish Uncle Joe's home. We hoped Estelle would return soon and take over some of the care of his restoration to health. Grandma was actually ill but would not give up. She coaxed Uncle Joe with strength-giving food and he was beginning to have more energy. But I felt he was worrying about his family. Grandma set her mouth in a grim line and spat her snuff into the fireplace. I could not tell if she would have preferred Estelle's return or not.

Father decided to try a late garden. Seed could be obtained now, and if the weather was favorable the lack of an early start might not matter. We planted beans, turnips, potatoes—both Irish and sweet—and pumpkins. Northern corn and butterbeans were very timely. We worked about the shop to restore it to condition and now and then managed to do some shop work, using Father's one good hand and both of mine.

It was quite an occasion the first day Uncle Joe was able to walk as far as the shop. We drank a toast of Grandma's grape wine to the health of us all. It was an occasion in more ways than one, for that evening a train of wagons arrived and unloaded, among other settlement wives and children, Estelle, Jane, and Jim.

It was after supper and we were seated around our front door. Estelle, leaving the kindly neighbor's wagon, came toward us. She was thin and worn, and pity welled in my heart. The sight of us so comfortable and clean made her face work with feelings she could not conceal. She stood, in all her fatigue, before us. The children ran to Uncle Joe and greeted him affectionately.

"Well, Joe Bratton, I suppose you fought to your finish and slunk home to your Ma to get well fed while your family waded the slick, murky waters of the river bottoms. I hope you've satisfied yourself. And you, Mis' Bratton—"

Grandma had risen to her greatest height and, taking the tired woman by both shoulders, plumped her down in the seat by Uncle Joe. Estelle was too horrified and surprised for utterance. The children began to cry.

"Just becalm yourself, Estelle Roan Bratton, and be sure you know what you're talking about. And another word out of you about any comforts will be pushed down your throat before you have any food. Now just sit quiet-like and we'll see what we can scrape together. But for your information, your own house has been reconditioned by these hands here and has been waiting for you to return."

Grandma went indoors and, thinking I would be needed, I also left. Father wandered down to the shop.

When I called Estelle in for supper, she seemed humbled but her eyes snapped as she watched Grandma's bent back before the fireplace, so I braced my shaking body against the table.

''Estelle.'' I was surprised at my own temerity, but forced her to look at me before I continued. ''We had suffering and deprivation, you and I, together. If you had more after you left us, it was your own choice. These people of ours have gone through more than you will ever know. Now is the time for you to make amends or to break what has been done. I warn you, step lightly.''

She sat at the table and ate in a manner that left no doubt of her hunger. And she did not say a word. Later she gathered her children to her and walked to the house without a word or a glance toward any of us. Uncle Joe started to follow, found his weakness still upon him, and sat down again. Later Father assisted him across the hundred yards or more to his home. We had no team. Dan and Ran were not returned.

To this day I do not know what transpired at that home-going. But Estelle slowly recovered her composure. Each day I went over with Uncle Joe's bowl of soup, quinine, and often other food. We sent milk and butter when needed. Our family was reunited at last.

18

WHEN UNCLE JOE'S health was improved to the point that he could eat solid food, Grandma took to her bed. I knew little of doctoring and tried to get her to advise me. But her illness was more the weakness of spirit. We did all we could to enliven her and she responded with her old manner, but I feared it was for our benefit. No one could know the depth of her thinking. However, she did improve and would not give way to her weakness.

"Actually I am ashamed to let little things like a month's war get me down," she said one day. "I must be getting old."

To my seventeen years, seventy-one seemed many, but I replied, "Grandma, you will never be old. Just realize that in you, age is only a matter of milestones in accomplishments. We have just begun to live. Texas is now what we had hoped to find and it is ours to make of it what we will.

"No," I shook my head—I was trying to speak sagely to impress her with the fact that I had grown to sufficient age to relieve her of some of her responsibilities—"you are not old, neither are you disappointed. You just need a little of the care, love, and food that you have bestowed on the rest of us. And you'll get it if you will just declare a few days' holiday and let me take over."

She drew me to her and placing a hand on each cheek, looked long into my eyes. I had not told her of Brentwood, but felt she knew something had happened.

"Stamina, that's what it is!" she almost gloated. "All right, child, the helm is yours for a few days."

I felt she slept that night. But memories crowded into my thinking to prevent my closing my eyes. During the long hours I, too, fought a battle and decided that one disappointment should not ruin a life of usefulness.

''Father,'' I approached him in the garden the next morning, as I began to help him weed the vegetables, ''I think I shall not want to leave home for school, at least not yet. Perhaps there is something I can do about a school here. Have you heard any mention of building a new schoolhouse?''

''Why, no, child. Do you think that Mr. Haynes is not coming back?''

''No, Father. I am sure he is not returning.''

''Well, it would be a wonderful idea for you to have a small group if you think you could do it.'' A twinkle came into his eyes and I knew he was thinking of my arithmetic.

''But if I had you and Grandma to help me at home evenings,'' I said, ''I might be able to learn and also teach at the same time. We would have books and I could study ahead. I think I should like to try it.''

For a moment I thought he was going to take me in his arms there in the garden patch. But he only held me tightly by the shoulders and said earnestly, ''That is a wonderful idea.''

19

I HAD THE PRIVILEGE of planning the school building. It would be in a new location and would be a larger room than the old one. Most of the homes were completed and the entire settlement turned out for the house-raising that would be our new church and school. The women cooked and brought dinner to spread under the trees. Now that there was more flour, and eggs were plentiful, cakes and pies prevailed on the menu, with beautiful loaves of bread. Meat was turkey and squirrel stew as cattle lost in the turmoil had not been replaced.

Two weeks' work was sufficient for the building. Father wanted to finish the interior himself. He made benches with slat bottoms so they would not be so hard, and polished the wood for the small pulpit. The floor was smooth oak. There was a huge fireplace on one side, with a beautifully carved mantle. I hoped to have a mirror over it before many months. Windows were shuttered, as it was too difficult to obtain glass ones. A small woodshed for extra wood and kindling was built to one side.

When it was all completed, in the late summer, our church-school building was duly dedicated to its high purpose with a prayer meeting. I spent much time gathering books to plan the course of study. I obtained ideas from other schools that were being held throughout the settlements, planning to work out simple lessons for the beginners and other courses according to the wishes or needs of the older people. I thought, with pain in my heart, that there would be no more long quotations of poetry, except for memory lessons.

Grandma and I had to see about new clothes for both of us. Calico had come to the trading post. Although it was very expensive, we had to buy it because there was no cotton to weave. I wore the blue dress only on rare occasions, although we had used Grandma's fichu to fill in the low neckline and it was more serviceable that way. Two calico dresses and my two or more old homespun ones seemed, to my excited eyes, to be quite an adequate wardrobe, as they hung in my corner of the bedroom near the little broken piece of mirror. Uncle Joe made some shoes for me out of the hides that had covered the splinters on our floor. These planks were being planed down, now, into beautiful shiny oak. The planing took off a lot of the greasy spots that had popped out or were spilled about the fireplace during our cooking—and which had not been removed by our scrubbing with ashes. We spread a bear rug before the fire, though, and our room began to take on the appearance of luxury.

It was time for the sugar and molasses mill to begin its work. The mill was reconditioned and the call went out over the settlements to bring in the cane. There would be very little of this product, however, and it seemed that our favorite confections were to be scarce. But it brought Neleetah to our door and that was quite a welcome sight.

"Neleetah!" I threw my arms about the huge neck.

"Hi!" His eyes gleamed but he stood like a statue, his arms folded.

"But no molasses, Neleetah," said Grandma, "although we hope to have some later."

"Neleetah no come molasses, need help. Steve want home."

"Steve! Where is he?" I exclaimed.

We waited for the slowly drawn answer.

"My home. Wounds well. Wants home."

I sank into the nearest chair.

Grandma was more steady of nerve. "And you need a cart to bring him, Neleetah, is that it? Surely. Yes. We have no team but one will be found and you can bring him right here."

"Steve no come Brattons. Wants home," was Neleetah's reply.

"All right, all right," said Grandma. "But first he comes here, tell him. So I can see that he is comfortable."

Neleetah shook his head. "No come here, betcha." The last word was a new one. His tongue dwelled on it.

I thought I knew the reason.

"Grandma, Father and I will go with Neleetah to bring Steve. But his home should be repaired so he will not feel so terrible about it. What shall we do?"

"Go get your father," said Grandma crisply.

Within an hour, kindly neighbors were working under Grandma's directions to repair Steve's little home. Weeds were cut down, fences repaired, floors scrubbed, and window shutters hung. Father and I accompanied Neleetah.

We found that his tent was pitched near the camp-meeting grounds. We crossed a small creek, fording it on its rocky botton. I heard a waterfall near by. As we drove up to the little tent, Neleetah commanded, "Wait."

We waited for some time, then Neleetah raised the flap which was his door and said, "Come."

I let Father go first and tried to steady my emotions when I entered and saw the wasted form on the pallet of skins and worn blankets. Steve's eyes were burning sockets in his face, and they found me at once. He frowned and I knew it was not the time for emotions, so I fought for control.

"I called Grandma a true Trojan," I said, "and she said I am a true Texan. You might be termed both, Steve"

"A mere fragment of the remains," he said gloomily. "No, really, in justice to Neleetah and my guardian angel, Albina, you find a specimen that is much improved over the one they picked up on the path out of Goliad."

"Goliad! *Stéve!*"

But his breath came in short gasps even with that little effort, so I heeded Neleetah's raised hand and said no more.

Grandma had sent some broth, rich with cream and potatoes, so I warmed it and fed Steve by spoonfuls. A Mexican woman came in and I was told it was she who had found Steve crawling slowly along a dry stream, bleeding from many wounds and crying for water, one of those miserable days after the massacre at Goliad. Only through the later years was I to learn how she bathed his face in water she had taken from a stream, then slowly let drops slide down his throat, how she carried him in her arms to a hidden cove in the creek bed, waiting for darkness because she would be killed, too, if found giving succor to an American in that territory. How, after darkness fell, she went for her husband and they took the wounded, unconscious boy on the back of a burro to their home, where, during the many days and nights of delirium in which Steve had called for his friends, the name which they best understood was the Indian name of Neleetah. She had bathed and dressed his wounds, giving him the herb teas she knew for fever.

Many days later, when news had come of the American victory for the Texas lands, they felt it would be an act in their favor to deliver the Texan to his friends. Then followed the long search for Neleetah and the tedious trip in a cart over rough roads through many rains. But Steve had been with Neleetah now for several weeks, and Trinidad and Albina Flores had made frequent trips to help in his convalescence. All this I learned in later days but now, when I first saw the tender administrations of Albina, I felt she had saved Steve's life. One Mexican woman had stolen my lover, but another had saved the life of a friend. It was not nationality that decided the issue, but personality and character, and I did not hold a grudge any longer, even against Therese.

Father and I decided that I should talk to Steve about staying with us. I knew more reasons for it than did Father and pondered over the best procedure.

''Steve,'' I said, on our slow journey home the next morning, ''we all want you at our home. Yours is all ready for you—cleaned up and waiting—but you know Grandma is not able to walk down there so often and she'll insist upon taking care of you. I shall want to help. So we hope you will agree to stop with us until you are able to care for yourself.''

He was silent for so long that I wondered if he were going to reply.

''You will think I am ungrateful,'' he said finally. ''It is more that I am ashamed. But I have to know one thing. Where—is—our former schoolteacher?'' He chose to say it that way.

''Brentwood?'' I was startled but had tried to prepare myself for some such inquiry. ''He will not be back,'' I replied. ''I happen to know that—he has married—and gone back to the states.''

Steve gave my hand a slight pressure but did not reply. When we arrived home, Uncle Joe assisted us in placing Steve in his old bed in Father's room. So Grandma added another patient to her list.

I left them and went down to Steve's home. I wanted to see how it looked. The transformation was wonderful. Steve could have appreciated it more if he had seen the wreckage before the neighbors had ministered to it. Until the dusk was thickening I sat on the doorstep, feeling the terror of the past weeks flow in endless waves through my consciousness and out into the night. At that time I knew little of Steve's story but to have him home at all was counted in my blessings of the year.

How kind is a providence that does not reveal to us the trials ahead except from day to day. What would have been our reaction to the call of duty, as it had come to us during the past weeks, had we known of the shadows in our pathway? How good that we did not know the future but were able, through the strength gained in the accomplishments of the past, to go forward without fear. That is true pioneering.

20

FATHER WANTED TO accompany me that first day of school and I felt I would need him very much. My knees were weak as I began my unusually careful toilet.

But Grandma said, "Let the child go alone. It would seem to others that she couldn't be sufficient unto herself. There are occasions when one feels he has not courage to face an issue without backing, but when the time comes I think Malinda will be all right."

I kissed them both and went to Steve's bedside. His face was solemn as he said, "Good luck, Texan," and my eyes filled with tears.

"Be boosting for me, Steve. I am not as full of courage as Grandma thinks. But I'll admit I am greatly excited. Perhaps that is all."

He pressed my hand in parting and I had the idea that he was thinking more of someone else than of me at the moment.

I rushed out and down the road to our new building. The early morning was thrilling, and was all that should be needed to urge one on to new ambitions. I wanted to go early to be ready for my pupils. I had gathered some goldenrod and Spanish mulberry to arrange in a blue bowl. It was the first of October; the air was dry and full of pungent odors. I opened the shuttered windows, placed the bowl of flowers on the mantle over the fireplace, arranged my books, and studied the plan I had worked out over the weeks.

Slowly, one by one, the children began to come in, their eyes wide with excitement, their attitude one of expectancy. It was obviously their first day in the schoolroom. They whispered together and followed my every movement. I tried to engage them in conversation but they only tucked their heads and, placing little clean hands over their mouths, giggled in fun. I was disappointed, when the time came to ring the bell at the front door, to find that only small children had appeared. There were about a dozen. Some mothers came, and later I found that one or two of them would like to attend classes. The speech of welcome I had planned hardly applied to such a group. I wondered if I could rise to the occasion as Grandma had said. So I tried to welcome them in manner suitable to their own knowledge and then we sang a song and had a prayer.

I asked the mothers to help me decide what the children should study. This created a cooperative interest and was worthwhile. But as we divided them into classes according to their former training, I thought I would hardly need the arithmetic, geography, and other studies that I had drilled myself to endure.

The day's work was over early and I went to Father's shop. When I saw the inquiring look on his face, I realized how disappointed I had been and felt like tears.

"Father, no one came except a few little children and some of their mothers."

He was silent a moment, then said, "You know, I believe that is a healthy sign."

"What do you mean?"

"Well, you see it shows they would not embarrass you by going from curiosity. They want to be sure, first, how you will manage. They may come in gradually and you will be able to get adjusted as you go along. Also, the older boys and girls are still very busy rebuilding their homes and gathering the little crop they were able to raise. You know, corn and cotton are late this year because of the delayed planting. Chin up, and you will find you are fortunate, don't you think?"

"As usual, your line of thought cheers me up, Father," I said, kissing him. "You see how I do need you. But I am glad you did not go this morning. I shall need you more when I get home."

As days grew into weeks there were many other additions to my classes and I found that Father was right. Several girls not much younger than I, large boys, and, later in the fall, three young men, a girl of fourteen, and another girl about seventeen years of age. I felt rather overwhelmed but we began in a spirit of comradeship and I tried to teach them on that basis. Singly, they often knew more than I did, but with the prestudying that I did at home with my family's help, I was still master of my ship.

But there was definitely a growing sense of jealousy and I did not know how to combat it. Some pupils naturally required more of my time, and the older boys and girls were quick to consider such in the light of partiality. They used this idea in a move to create dissension and a division of purpose among themselves. I spoke to Father about it.

"There should be some organization among the parents," he said, "to which you could appeal when questions of controversy arise."

He talked to others and they selected four men of the community to act as a board. Father was not one of them. I felt much more comfortable and for a time the atmosphere seemed clear of friction.

Steve was my great comfort in the preparation of lessons. I learned to like history and geography but felt that most subjects other than reading, writing, and proper speech were a waste of time. I had many goodhumored discussions with my family in their well-meaning effort to prevent my programs from being overbalanced in those studies.

Supervision grew more difficult for me as time passed. There were ever new problems arising which called for immediate answers. Some of these seemed directed at me personally, a kind of test or examination on the part of my students. I thought there was a distinct aversion to the idea of the board of adults, as though it were the result of an inadequacy on my part. Small groups gathered on the playgrounds in deep conversation which broke abruptly when I approached. I knew that some pupils were withdrawing from my confidence, although many others were not. But there seemed to be nothing to use as a basis for recovery of the understanding I had thought we had established. I felt frustrated and helpless and was comforted only by the fact that while a definite group carried on such activities, the others took no part in the intrigue.

One small boy, Charlie Hobbs, came each day from some distance. He was accompanied by his faithful dog, Cap. Cap became our watchdog, barking when there was undue approach to our door. He soon learned who were parents or neighbors.

But Cap had one bad habit. He did not know that school kept, and always had his nose to the scent of a rabbit or squirrel. When he had trailed one of these small animals to a hollow log or tree, he kept up an insistent barking until the school was keyed for the hunt. Charlie would duck his head and look embarrassed, but one day the other boys persuaded me to let them go find Cap's victim.

Across to the woods went boys and all to bring out the animal. There was quite a sport of it, in cutting through the log or cutting the tree and finding the game. At times the girls joined in the chase but they were mostly interested in the ripe huckleberries. The blue juice of that fruit was a telltale evidence on lips and hands when they returned.

Very little study was possible after such adventures, but I hoped at least to create a better feeling of comradeship and friendly relations.

It soon became evident that some of the children were not included in these exploits, whether from their own choice or oversight on my part, I did not know. From this fact came a revealing knowledge. Dora Meeks and her brother, John, had created a nucleus of another crowd. They were of a family who long had been a part of Hill Grande but whose parents had been dubbed "dissenters" by most of our settlement. They seldom agreed with others and became more and more a problem to the neighborhood. I had wondered about the children.

Dora was very homely but also very brilliant. Seldom did she need prompting in any way and I had not realized this would cause her to be unpopular with her companions. As a result she seemed to build a wall of reserve about herself and to take little part in any activities of the school. John stood by his sister faithfully, although, being less shy, he followed the hunters on their rounds and joined in the games of the play periods.

One day some of the other girls declined to go on the hunt because of the severe cold. I was deep in lesson plans and had not heard or realized the discussion—which had grown to a debatable point—until I heard Dora say, "Ma says there ought to be more did at school than is doin' here, huntin' rabbits and sich, if'n Mis' Bratton knowed her teachin' like she ought. Ma 'spects to take us out to chop cotton come spring."

"Well," said the other girl, "that shouldn't teach you a lot."

"Whut's learnin' got to do with it?" asked Dora. "Nuthin' but pettin' that Hobbs boy and his dog. Ma says she needs us at home worse'n that."

"Well, Dora, suppose we just study while the Hobbs boy and his dog learn the art of the chase," I said.

I smiled, although I did not feel like it. There probably was more of such conversation on the playgrounds. Some of those who had gone hunting were capable of the same ideas. I felt the problem was with the parents. What had Grandma once said? "People from every state, nation, and across the seas." Differences of ideas and opinions, yet being molded into one group and one neighborhood. No wonder the children felt it—no wonder there were diversities of thought.

I should have been forewarned. But I decided to view the incident as idle gossip and did not mention it to Father.

One day Charlie brought a note from his mother asking if I would come with her son some evening and spend the night. Since I was not of the usual teacher program—boarding about in the homes—I felt it was a friendly gesture, and when I talked it over with my family, we decided I should go. It might be well to try to visit in all the homes, either overnight or some evening. So I trudged with Charlie, or rather tried to keep up with him and Cap, over the mile to his home as the two of them scampered through the autumn woods, ignoring trails, but coming out true point to a small two-room log house not very far away.

I had expected criticism on the part of Charlie's parents, perhaps on the freedom of my school program. During our supper of fried squirrel and hot corn pones, however, little conversation was permitted. That, introduced chiefly by myself, drew short answers and then silence. Charlie tried to tell of his experiences but was hushed calmly by his father. I decided that the silence was through politeness for the visitor and that consuming the meal was the principle project of the moment.

When Charlie's father had pushed his plate far into the table and his chair as far back, conversation commenced in a lively manner. I learned much of interest of the Hobbs family and they asked many questions of the settlement life. They had come from Connecticut about two years previously and were interested in all the activities of our community but had been too busy and, perhaps, too shy to enter into them. I invited them to our next singing bee and learned that Mr. Hobbs had a wonderful bass voice.

Charlie and I reached school on time the following morning. Quite a group had gathered at the schoolroom door to watch our approach. The thought of an unusual interest in my overnight visit in Charlie's home hit me with a feeling of foreboding. But the greetings were as a whole cheerful and friendly. I hastened to my desk to arrange my work for the morning, already feeling the lack of preparation the evening before.

How could I have doubted a friend? There on my desk, in Steve's scrawling handwriting, was a folded paper—inside, the day's mathematics problems! I was flushed with gratitude as I rang the bell for assembly.

Early in the afternoon I began to feel an unusually hushed quality in the silence of the schoolroom. I continued the lessons with an uneasy sensation of increased foreboding. Perhaps I was in haste to get back to my home with the good report of my visit, for, the day's work completed, I closed the room for the night and waited about with less than my usual patience until all students were on their way home.

When I glanced about the grounds for what should have been the final time, I discovered, to my surprise, a group of boys and men at the back of the building. There, lying on the ground, was the still form of a dog. It was Cap. Kneeling by his side, trying to rouse his pal, was Charlie, crying as though his heart would break. I looked to the other boys for an explanation but most of them slipped quietly away. Two of Charlie's friends, Chip Goodwin and Fred Sharp, knelt with Charlie and, looking into my face accusingly, said, "Cap's poisoned."

"Oh, no!" I cried. "Who could poison a dog—a dumb animal?"

"He wan't dumb!" cried Charlie.

My heart ached for the boy.

All was confusion, as parents and grown people about the trading post heard of the tragedy and came toward us. Father came. He and Steve hitched our horse to the cart and placed the dog gently into it. We all went home with Charlie and his dead friend. I felt there was no explanation I could make to the parents or their heartbroken boy but my feeling of foreboding returned.

Father shook his head when I told him the full story and we decided it was a matter for the board. If such acts were possible for our boys and girls, what might be the future of our men and women? We called a meeting of the board for noon the next day.

Mr. Rogers was chairman and wished to question the pupils. But only profound silence answered the questions. There was just no response. I told them of the several hunts which I had permitted as recess periods, and added that I felt the boys would benefit by the outing, and that the privilege had been open to all and had not been abused by the pupils. All the boys agreed that Cap had been a friend to everyone.

Charlie's parents were present. Mr. Hobbs arose and asked to speak. "Cap's dead," he said. "But the folks of the settlement are alive and we live together. There's no call for unfriendliness because of one mistake. Someone is sorry now for having done this act. It'll hurt him worse than it'll hurt the rest of us, unless we let a cantankerous act, done on the spur of the moment of madness, eat out our own better judgment. It was a mean act, I'll admit. But we must forgive and forget. It seems this group," he looked about the room at the awed students, "has a good trait—loyalty. So let's let them benefit by this loyalty and hope it prevents worse tragedies in the future. I am willing to forget and hope Charlie can. But," he looked down at his son who cried softly on his mother's shoulder, "give the boy a few days. He is really cut deep."

Mr. Rogers dismissed the assembly and everyone crowded about the Hobbs family. Many of the children scampered out, others were trying to reach Charlie's side, when a loud voice arose over the others, saying:

"Just a minute, please. I want to take somethin' up at this meetin' here."

The group was electrified into silence and turned with one accord to where Mrs. Meeks stood in the back of the room. My first thought was that she surely must have missed Mr. Hobbs' speech.

Mr. Rogers spoke. "Why, good morning, Mrs. Meeks. I had not noticed you were here. What is it you want?"

"Wal, now, Mr. Rogers, you all have hired Miss Bratton here to teach our chillun. I ain't the one to say huntin' is the thing to do in school time but mine has got plenty to do at home. I ain't a woman of schoolin', but I do try to have my boy and my girl with the best of folks.

"That dog was causing trouble in the schoolroom all the time and Miss Bratton would turn out the whole bunch to hunt. We don't go to school at my house to learn to hunt when I need my children at home to help farm and chop wood. I had Dora give that dog the poison to try to stop the foolishness quiet-like. Seems it didn't turn out like that. I don't want any more trouble. Maybe I was wrong. Dora, she didn't want to do it."

She looked over at Charlie, who was crying even louder after the confession. "I'll git the boy another dog," she offered.

"I should say you will," a loud voice, that of a pupil, exclaimed.

With that, the room was filled with an uproar, but silence fell as Mr. Rogers stood, holding up both hands for quiet, looking out at the faces before him. One by one the people in the schoolroom began to look at each other and then at the floor as the charged atmosphere in the room began to change. Each person present was remembering that Ed Meeks had died at the seige of the Alamo, while those accusing his family now were alive only because they were not on the fighting front that early in the war.

"Does anyone want to place a charge against Mrs. Meeks?" asked Mr. Rogers.

Silence filled the room.

"Well, there is a motion to adjourn this meeting."

Everyone rose and quietly left the room. But I noticed Mr. Rogers and another trustee talking to Mrs. Meeks about the board visiting with her and the children later, in her home.

Afterward, Mr. Rogers told me and Father that there was a congenial feeling in the Meeks home, and that he felt that every phase of pioneer living, and the laws governing one's neighborly conduct toward his neighbor, had been fully explained and understood.

I could hardly conceive of the proceedings at the time, but it had cleared the atmosphere of many things for future thinking. For myself I knew my solution would be not to decide on the guilt of a person, but rather to create a more kindly and understanding attitude toward a lonely family. The entire community seemed to feel the effect of that experience for a long time. And it surely was the beginning of a new era in Hill Grande.

21

A CLOSER RELATIONSHIP among the parents and young people of our neighborhood was needed. I planned activities to use our new school building for community affairs, encouraging more social gatherings, more meetings for singing and prayer services. Uncle Joe was slowly recovering from the malaria and I persuaded him to organize singing bees. We moved the old organ out to the school building, but I think we were happier with Uncle Joe's tuning fork. Spelling matches were enjoyed by the young and old, the older folk because it gave them an opportunity to brush up on their knowledge from earlier training, the younger ones because it gave them a chance to put onto a challenging basis what they had learned during their intermittent school days.

There would be no camp meeting for awhile, although our hearts were more grateful than ever. Unsettled conditions made such a gathering dangerous as it would leave homes and stock without ample protection against attacks of bands of marauders and roaming Indians. Perhaps the war had made us supersensitive to danger. Also the men were not willing to expose their women and children to such discomforts as were necessary at the camp-meeting grounds when it was possible to have our spiritual programs at home. A visiting preacher now and then held weekly services in our schoolhouse, and when the crowd overflowed its benches, the evening services were held out under the trees in the town square. Prayer meetings were regular Wednesday evening occurrences. Singing bees and spelling matches were almost every Saturday night's social gatherings. Our spiritual growth advanced with our town's advancement, and to its improvement.

Uncle Joe had secured an old violin in some kind of a trade. He and Jim entertained the village boys and girls for some time around their household doorstep while they all sang to the rather rasping accompaniment of the "fiddle." Jim Roan had revealed a very good singing voice and he had no timidity in singing out to the loudest and highest notes of the hymnals.

I chose others of the children's singing group and, by placing similarly toned voices together, was able to arrange quite a chorus. I hoped to teach them the words correctly, and perhaps something of inflection and phrasing as I knew it. Our only source for words of the tunes that everybody knew and loved were the handwritten copies of songs, mostly made during the early days. Many were in Brentwood's handwriting originally, and others were copies we had made during the school days as he "lined out" the songs during our lesson period. The sight of the familiar handwriting made my eyes smart, but, I thought, there could be no better memorial of the service he might have contributed to our community than these songs, so typical of his troubadour spirit.

There were never enough copies of these songs to go around, so naturally the children sang from memory and from their understanding of the words as sung by their elders. Little wonder, then, that Jane refused to sing of "the seatless love of our Savior," nor that when Jim's clear loud voice declared, "My Savior's cross-eyed bear," which was his interpretation of the sounds that came to him, he often seemed to suppress a grin. I felt it was time well spent when we compiled a songbook from copies gathered from the various homes, arranging the songs in a uniform manner. There was always much commotion and loss of time while everyone found the words to the same song. It was several years before we owned a real hymnal in our church.

Jim and Jane were much impressed with the singing groups and were ardent members of my chorus. They included their knowledge of it all in their "play preachin' "—their favorite manner of entertaining other children of the neighborhood. Jim would mount a tree stump in his role as preacher while Jane directed the choir. When the mournful sound of their singing reached a certain pitch, their old black dog, Shep, always raised his head to the skies and howled as though he was part of the program. And well he was, as Jim and Jane called his contribution their organ. Their mother wanted to punish them for being sacriligious, but Uncle Joe intervened, saying it was a very worthy and instructional play for them.

Postal service was much improved with the better stage lines, and, as a consequence, we had many evenings for reading and study groups. Not everyone received the newspapers, so it was interesting to read what papers there were together, and to discuss the happenings of our government as well as to receive news of the other Texans and of the outside world. General Houston was now our president—President of the Texas Republic!

But in December we were saddened by the death of our benefactor, Stephen F. Austin, and the entire republic was in mourning during the holidays.

And in the meantime the situation with Mexico remained unsettled, and the continuous calls for volunteers made for an unrelenting feeling of unrest and insecurity.

22

MY HOURS WERE FULL and happy ones. I felt I was creating a place in Hill Grande's future for myself and seldom did I dwell on the past, certainly never on my love for Brentwood. One day, however, I was forced to recall it because of a conversation among my older pupils before our fire.

"I did not go to school when he taught here, so I didn't know him, but from the tales that are told, he must have been quite a character."

I was busy arranging papers for the lessons to follow, but the words attracted my attention.

"Well, he wasn't quite the fighter he thought he was, evidently," another voice added, "or he wouldn't have tried a trip through those East Texas Indians with no more protection than a Mexican servant. All that fancy-trappings that he married, too, only added to the kill."

I sat down, suddenly too weak to stand, but managed to ask, "What story are you boys talking of now, Philip?"

"Oh, you know that man who taught here, Mr.—What's his name, Haynes? Married that rich Spanish woman in San Antonio? Well, they tried to get out of the country to the Louisiana line but the Indians got them."

"He was a traitor, anyway," said another, "or he wouldn't have left the country like that. At least, not then."

I heard no more, as I fainted.

As I revived, I felt water being splashed over my face and anxious pupils were all about us. Someone had gone for Father. He dismissed school and gave me a drink of the whiskey he kept in the shop. For some time he would not let me speak. The children in their excitement had told him of their conversation when they saw me slide out of my chair, so he did not need an explanation.

Later, as we sat before the fire, I asked, "Father, it cannot be true?"

"My child, it is the story we have heard. It probably has gathered embellishment with each telling. We had hoped you would be spared. You loved him, did you not?"

I could only nod my head.

"There are other stories you may hear, so let's clean house on it all now," he added. "Brentwood Haynes had been accused of bearing messages for both the patriots and the Mexicans. The woman he married influenced him beyond his own good. He probably married her for her money and as a means of escape. I fear he was more of an adventurer than we would like to believe. Your grandmother and I have worried about you often, Malinda. I hope you will not let this influence the future affairs of your heart. Did you know he was married?"

"Oh, yes," and I told him of my experience at Groce's Ferry. "I think I have not loved him since that time, but this just seems so tragic, more final. And I can never love anyone and be hurt like that again!"

"My dear child, he was far from being worthy of the suffering and the embarrassment he caused you. You must forget it all—put it behind you—and not let such an experience influence you with a more worthy person, as I feel sure you will know some day, if not now.

"Come," he arose and lifted me to my feet. "Grandma will wonder what has happened to both of us." Then only did I realize that the sun was going down.

That evening when I went for Bossy, I stood under my oak tree for the first time in many months. I tried to wash from my heart all the bitterness I had felt for Brentwood and Therese. I wanted to remember the hours I had with him. All through my life they would be my romance, my first love. To him I must have been only a part of his love for life, for adventure, and for a foremost place in any episode.

That evening Steve took to his bed immediately after supper and I found studying much removed from my thoughts. I went to sleep far into that night, not thinking but trying to forget to think. The next day at school the pupils looked askance, as though they sought an explanation. I could only beg their forgiveness for folding up on them and promised to be more stable in the future. I seemed to be one of those people who could be as stalwart as Grandma in a major crisis, but who had trouble coping with the less demanding ones.

"We just must not tell such harrowing stories in front of ladies," said Philip.

I thought it best to leave it that way.

Grandma did not mention the cause of my faint but gave me a small bottle of smelling salts which she had not used for years to carry with me.

"And don't keep that schoolroom so stuffy," was her only comment.

And well it might have been caused by the foul air, because the boys chewed their tobacco and spat into the ashes of the fire during school hours. Two of the older girls dipped snuff. I had been accustomed to Grandma's moderate use of snuff, but had never thought women were very neat with tobacco and did not intend forming the habit myself. I had tried it, of course, as every girl had, but Steve and I decided that smoking the grapevine stem was a nicer and more pleasant diversion and that was the extent of our use of the weed in our childhood play.

Tobacco became one of our neighborhood's principal crops, however. The next spring's planting was abundant. Uncle Joe and Father had cleared more land, and during the summer Steve, who had not been able to do much preparation, worked the crops Father had planted for him. He also cut trees and cleared land, split rails to build fences, and, in the exercise, developed strong muscles in the place of the weakened, wounded limbs.

A post office was named for Hill Grande and Uncle Joe was made postmaster. It was a wonderful opportunity for him, and Estelle beamed with pride. They added a little store with a small line of merchandise and she spent most of her time there. Father was very busy in his blacksmith shop as it was quite a task to keep all the plows and tools repaired for the growing populace, as well as all the horses shod and guns in order. Paper money, called "red backs," came into use and trade and bartering became a matter of convenience only, and not a necessity.

We had chickens and guineas that fall and Uncle Joe had some pigs. Father traded a pony from Mr. Ryan and gave it to me. I was most happy. I rode for the first time to Sophie's. We seldom had a visit anymore and I missed her companionship. Uncle Joe made a sidesaddle for me, but until it was finished I rode sideways on a man's saddle, which was not very comfortable. During that autumn, each Saturday afternoon I practiced riding, and Steve usually accompanied me. We took new trails leading into the hills. I learned to ride downhill without holding the horn of my saddle in fear. Horseback riding became our chief sport.

I sometimes thought of those daring pony express riders, who used to bring us our mail whenever they could. It seemed so long ago—and yet it had been only a few short years. Now Uncle Joe was postmaster, the mail came fairly regularly by stage, and I was riding a horse just for sport!

23

GRANDMA'S HEALTH FAILED considerably during the winter months. It was apparent to all of us that she was not recovering in her usual manner from the anxious days of the war. Such suffering had sapped her reserve strength, and she would not admit the true state of her feelings sufficiently to permit proper treatment that would allow her complete return to health. Father felt that our home was becoming inadequate and should be more comfortable. All during the winter months he and Steve worked on materials for a new home to be built in the spring. Steve also began to work with Father in the shop and it became established that he would help there when needed.

We planned a tree for Christmas and a program in the schoolroom. It was to be quite a gala occasion. The tree was a beautiful cedar and the pungent odor, warmed by the fire in the great fireplace, filled the room. For days the pupils spent much time making paper-ring chains and stringing popcorn to be used in decoration. Evergreen garlands hung from the ceiling, the mantle was banked with greens—wild smilax vine, yupon berries, and cedar. Candles were placed in every available spot, to be lighted at the last moment. I trained the small children in songs and recitations. The older folks, led by Uncle Joe, would sing carols. The little room could not contain all the people who would want to come, so we built an arbor outside the door, covering it with cedar branches for protection against the cold wind.

That evening before Christmas Eve, Steve and I went down to light the candles and get the full effect. It was beautiful. Gifts had begun to arrive to be placed under the tree the next day. On the tiptop of the cedar was a figure of a Christmas angel which had been used in our family each

Christmas for many years. It was white and shiny, just above the glow of the candles, and added a solemnity to the gaiety of the lower branches.

I stood gazing at it in awe and exclaimed, "Steve, did you ever see anything so beautiful?"

He did not answer and I turned to see where he was. He stood close at my side, and the expression on his face, which was bent to mine, was one that stirred my memory. I blushed, for I had forgotten that day in the old schoolroom. But I searched what I could remember and thought I had surely been busy with my own affairs not to have realized how Steve felt toward me. I think I am honest in saying that it had never occurred to me that he loved me. He took my hands.

"Linda." It was a whisper. "I am still waiting."

I withdrew my hands and went to the fire, trying to find an answer in its steady blaze. Then I turned to Steve.

"Then wait a little while longer, Steve, will you? I really did not know—"

"But there's hope, Linda? That is what I need so much to feel I may have."

"Hope?" Would I disappoint him? I could not endure that. "Why, Steve, that is what I need to find in my own heart. I had never thought of our lives as being anything other than a friendship. But," I half-laughed, nervously, "I surely would not want to be deprived of that."

He pushed me down, gently, into a chair by the fire and, seating himself before me, took both of my hands in his, and said, "Linda, may I tell you what I think love is? What it means to me? What it takes to make a lasting happy association of one man with one woman?"

I could hardly bring my gaze into focus with two eyes so earnest and pleading, for mine were wavering and uncertain. But he continued.

"Love is the natural feeling that comes to a man or woman, or both, after years of association that make thoughts and ideas, ambitions and aspirations, as one, that make mutual understanding as natural as the routine of a day, that brings desire for completion of the years they have already spent together in a long-lasting life with a home and children, and the united continuation of the things they have begun separately.

"You have had a more complete home than I, but we both know the sacredness of it. How do you think I could look forward to a life without you by my side? You and Grandma have spoiled me. You will have to continue in it. My childhood with you has grown into this love for you, the desire for you as my wife. I ask for your hand, Linda. Your father and grandma have given me their consent."

He stood now, looking down at the top of my head, holding out his hands. At that moment, voices came to us in Christmas carols. A group of my children were outside and I remembered telling them we would go caroling. I knew a great happiness but yet it was confused with uncertainty and newness. I arose and stood with my hands at my side.

"Dear Steve, I give you hope," I said, "but let me have time to learn about this new status for your life and mine. I think you are right, but I would not want to come to you with half my heart. I must be sure."

Steve looked crestfallen and hesitant.

"Come," I said, "I told those children you and I would accompany them caroling."

I tried to assure him with my smile, which trembled in spite of my efforts at self-control. He shook his shoulders as though removing a garment and followed me out into the night.

Steve and I had many happy associations during the following months. We worked together, rode together, sang and played together during the evening hours.

As soon as the spring planting had been completed and the weather settled down into April sunshine, Father and Steve went to work on our new home. It was to be built in front of the old one and would be connected to the two original rooms by a hallway. The old rooms, after being repaired, would be the storeroom and the kitchen. The new home would be a two-storied house with a gallery all the way across the lower front, a hallway down the center, and fireplaces both upstairs and down on each end. The downstairs rooms were to be of paneled oak, the upstairs bedrooms papered in some of the new wallpaper. Similar homes were being built in the vicinity and Father had helped with all of them. This one would be his pride and joy.

I spent much time waiting on the builders and trying to relieve Grandma of the excitement and noise. She spent more and more time in bed but followed the progress of the new home each day, and planned the milk house. We decided we needed some new furniture and that Grandma and I would go to New Orleans to choose it. Travel would be hard for her, however, and the summer days were already hot upon us. July brought intense heat and dry dusty roads which would be very trying, so we postponed our trip. In August the exterior of the new home was nearing completion. Father would work on the interior during his leisure, and we could move in to its new luxurious rooms gradually.

Despite all the newness around us, the renewal of spring and summer, and the growth of Hill Grande, there were those among us—and very dear to us—who were weakening, failing, and slowly slipping away.

Steve had told me sometime in June that he found it necessary to go to see about Neleetah every day or so. The old Indian was failing fast. He sat in one position in his tent, sometimes crawling to the door. There Steve often found him, nodding in his half-stupor, slowly grinding out the last sands of his years.

Then one day Steve came for Father and they went with several other men and laid our friend away to rest, burying with him the worn tent and his few other belongings. We had lost a good friend and a great protector. For some reason I superstitiously believed that now our barrier against Indian attacks was gone forever.

Uncle Joe was trying to conceal from his mother the steady development of a harrowing cough. His life in the store, his food—consisting chiefly of the cold products of his own merchandise—and his lack of any customary outdoor exercise—all of these were taking their toll of the constitution made weak by his experience with malaria. I felt I had to persuade him to confide in me.

"Uncle Joe, where did you get such a cough?"

"Malinda, I'm terribly worried but I can't think it's permanent. Could it be consumption?" His eyes were large and sunken from worry in his thin face. "I don't want Mother to know, and that's the reason I don't go to see her any oftener. Estelle thinks it's only a cold. I surely hope so."

"You shouldn't stay so closely in this store," I said. "Sunshine and fresh air are good cures. Why don't you go to a doctor?"

"Guess I could, but I hate to think of a trip all the way to Groce's just to have him tell me there's nothing you can do once you've got consumption."

"Bosh! Of course there is. Just tell him to give you something. Why don't you try some horehound tea and drink more of those iron-giving things that Grandma used to make. I think I'll just go and prepare you something myself." I hugged his neck. "Just can't see ole Josephus get thin and skinny," I mimicked, and kissed him on his forehead. It was clammy with perspiration.

I was at the fireplace making some potato soup when Grandma raised up to ask, "How's Joe feeling, Malinda? I haven't seen him for several days."

"Oh, I think all right, Grandma, just starving himself in that store. I told him I was going to bring him some food."

" 'T'ain't just that," she replied, "It's lack of appetite. That's what that gallopin' consumption does for one."

"Grandma!" I exclaimed.

"Well, he's got it. That's what his Pa died of." She lay back down on her pillow, continuing, "Of course, he doesn't know I know it. Tell him to come on and quit trying to fool me."

Even under the tragic circumstances, I could not help smiling. Trying to fool Grandma!

24

THE AUTUMN WAS AS gorgeous as usual. School and home duties and Grandma's need for my help left little time for outdoor pleasures. Steve and Father insisted upon the Saturday rides, however, and usually late in the afternoons we found our familiar trails over the hills and back. It no longer seemed an exertion to ride my lovely pony.

Now and then we rode to Sophie's and had a picnic under their trees, enjoying Johnnie's frolic with their little boy. I could see Steve's interest in their play and that, as much as anything, sealed around my heart the assurance that the life he desired would be a happy one for us both. But he did not press me for an answer, and so busy were we in caring for our loved ones that it seemed it would be selfish to plan for our own lives. I now realize that we deprived Grandmother of what would have been her greatest moment, but I feel she understands, as always, and will forgive me that mistake.

Early one morning Hill Grande was awakened by the rumble of many wagons and the creaking of yokes on oxen. Eight wagons rolled down the narrow dusty road that was our street—four new families were on their way to select homes in the new Republic! The village menfolk crowded about the tired drivers, children ran hurriedly to peep into the occasion, the women stood about their doors, listening, searching, for a familiar voice or face from "back home."

And, with a shout of welcome, Father was calling to Grandma, "It's the Simpsons, Mother! Grady, Belle, and all the folks!"

What a reunion it was! Our neighbors from back in Tennessee! Homesick years rolled across our vision and tears sprang to our eyes, Grandma's and mine, as we embraced Belle and her two daughters, Mary and Marg. There were now two small boys, Jack and Phil. I could not realize that Mary and Marg could be so grown up! But, as we laughed and looked at each other, I realized that of course, so was I! Grandma and Belle talked, interrupting each other with questions. The girls helped me with breakfast. But no one thought of food. All was glorious confusion.

The Simpsons had been ready to come to Texas when the news of the Revolution had reached Tennessee, and so had bided their time until rumors of the wonderful opportunities of the new Republic encouraged them to make the trip. They had been on the road two months and had met with many trials through the untracked forests and river bottomlands. There were two young men in the group who had scouted ahead, and when there were signs of trouble they had changed their course. They had reached Harrisburg in this roundabout journey and had then come back to Groce's to be directed to our settlement.

Grady Simpson said, "This Hill Grande should be called 'Haven for Travelers.' I think, if there is room for us, we'll just hitch onto your town."

Four new homes to build! Four new families to enfold into our living! The next day was Sunday and it was unanimously declared by Hill Grande as a day of prayer and feasting. The entire village spread its food upon the grounds of the square. I think I felt most happy for Grandma and Father, although Uncle Joe's eyes shone with a new twinkle and his shoulders squared with a purposeful mien. They each took pride in showing the Republic of Texas to our new friends from back home.

The young folk, too, were quite an asset to our daily living. We had grown too much to ourselves. We had not expanded from our family circle in a very broad sense. Life's activities around Hill Grande rose in rapid sequence with the arrival of the new group. I was happy to have young unmarried companions. Sophie and I were as fond of each other as always, but she was greatly occupied with her baby and her husband. Also, the young men, Paul Gray and Daniel Pound, were friendly and jovial additions to the younger male set of our community.

Mary and Marg, twin sisters though they were, had grown into quite different types of personalities. Marg was boisterous and gay, brown of hair and eyes, and dark of skin. Mary was quiet and reserved, beautifully blonde, and petite. It was evident from the beginning that the two girls were very much interested in Paul and Dan. There seemed promises of many thrilling adventures and experiences.

The foursome joined Steve and me in our riding expeditions, and we lost no time in showing them the wonders of our countryside. We often rode over the hills, down the pasture trails, and across the prairies.

Hunting trips were a natural activity during the fall season and early winter. Steve taught me to shoot more accurately, and Marg was good at all sports. But Mary usually sat her horse and held her hands over her ears, with her eyes closed, when a gunshot was forthcoming. We seldom went home empty-handed, and the succeeding fun of baking a wild turkey, cooking a pot of squirrel stew, or barbecuing a deer was something that even Mary enjoyed.

New homes for the four families were fast in construction, so many hands lent themselves to the task. Mr. Gray and Mr. Pound had planned to have a sawmill and came with materials to establish that industry. Those supplies helped in the construction of their own homes as well as those of their neighbors. The busy noises of the saw attracted the older settlers, and the sawmill was the center of interest for some time. Grady Simpson hoped to have a store of general merchandise. The other family, the Samuel Joneses, were farmers, and with Dan's help they planned some fine breeds of cattle and horses.

A sawmill would also make Father's work lighter as he could get materials there without having to prepare them himself. I had worried about him for some time now as it was impossible for him to turn a neighbor away from the shop after he had ridden miles to get work done. Often a man came in and shod his own horse, and that was good. I found excuses to remain around after school hours and often pumped the bellows and pushed the red-hot irons about, into the glowing coals. Now, with Steve's help and with prepared materials for the shop and the new home under construction, I felt relieved.

A long shed was built for storing the sawed lumber. The young folk of the settlement, and older ones, too, initiated it with a dance. Uncle Joe came with his fiddle and we danced to his music until he was exhausted. Then we discovered a fiddler in Daniel Pound! Our future enjoyment for frequent dances was ensured. Later, the need for a hall that was separate and apart from the church-school building was felt, and some of the first lumber prepared by the new sawmill was used for its construction. Homes were too small for our enlarged social gatherings. We felt very happy in the possession of the hall.

It became an effort for me to continue the community meetings and not feel that in doing so I was neglecting Grandma and home duties. And in November, Uncle Joe took to his bed. I could not go to those memorable singsongs without him.

We met in study groups and now had many stimulating discussions on problems of our Republic. The question of annexation with the United

States was quite a controversial one, and voices really rose. At times it seemed such a movement was assured, then it would recede again. Hill Grande was divided in opinion. The United States hesitated to assume the debt of the colonies—that contracted in our fight for freedom—and perhaps it hesitated also because of the hold that Mexico still claimed it rightfully had on its settlements in Texas. Yet—with all our vast acres of unimproved land! Our people were of the United States and annexation would seem like going home. It would alleviate local problems—it might solve our difficulties with Mexico. Perhaps time would work a cure, as Grandma always said. It was too complicated for my inexperienced mind to decide.

Christmas was quiet. The parents of my school wanted to present a play and I helped them all I could. It was a beautiful manger scene and we had Sophie for the mother, with a small baby as the Christ child. That, with Christmas carols, made a lovely program.

As we walked home that night, Steve and I stopped far enough away from the new home to see it in its entirety. Tall and stately, compared with the cabin that had been our abode for so long, I could not realize it would be ours, nor that it belonged to Texas. Somehow the log house seemed more fitting among the massive sturdy oaks and the rail fences of our surroundings. Father intended to spend the winter completing the beautiful carving and woodwork of the interior.

"Shall you ever want to leave it, Linda?" asked Steve.

"Oh!" I realized this was our moment. "You are helping build it, Steve. Is it not to be yours, too?"

"That is for you to decide, Linda. I would so much like to have you tell me tonight that you love me."

An owl down in the forest chose that moment to sing out "Who-o-o-ar!" But Steve heard my answer, and we were not frightened by a hoot owl there in the shadow of our future home.

Epilogue

IT IS WELL THAT the divine plan provides something new now and then in the life of man to prevent a feeling of complacency. I was too upset with Grandma's continued weakness and Uncle Joe's slow submission to his illness to keep informed as to our statehood. I tried to train Estelle in the art of soups and teas. She did not seem to bother too much over and above the usual food for her family, and Uncle Joe now had to be tempted to consume the food necessary to preserve his strength.

Grandma forced herself to help me in these added duties. I would be glad when school could be adjourned, as I knew well what the effect would be if I should quit my post. So, when Steve told me of the new threat to our peaceful Hill Grande, it was hard for me to produce the stamina to continue with my duties. The native Indians, incensed by the inroads being made on their lands by the ever growing number of colonists, incited also to a great extent by the dissatisfied Mexican authorities, were on an uprising. Several communities not far from our home had been wiped out by these raids. Could Hill Grande hope to go unscathed? With the loss of Neleetah, we had no ambassador. My feeling of superstition might well have been taken as a presentiment.

Father left the work on our home and spent all available time at the shop getting guns and ammunition in readiness. Word had been sent to President Lamar that protection was needed. Walls were built about the fort for a final stand. But our homes were too scattered for a general protection. And there stood our new home! Had we built it only for the torch?

I could not afford to show worry as we tried our best to keep this new excitement from Grandma's ears. She must be kept in peace. Finally it was Jane, Estelle's child, who brought the news to her in her childish prattle.

"I felt sure that would be our next trial," was Grandma's remark.

"Trial, Grandma?" I asked. I was in the room at the time and had hurriedly sped Jane on her way.

"Yes, my child," said Grandma. "In the chiseling of a new land out of a raw one, there are steps that must be endured. We have been very blessed in living through several. I feel that God will lead us safely through this. It will not be the last. We have always to keep vigil and not be found sleeping at the post. I suppose your father is getting guns and ammunition ready?"

"Yes, Grandma," I said, feeling defeat.

"Now, my child, don't show the weakness of crying! It's time to put away those easy tears you sometimes show. You and Steve will carry on, don't fear. This much preparation for a future is not so easily destroyed by a ravaging mind."

She had been very happy when Steve and I had told her of our plans. She wanted us to marry soon but so far we had not arranged it.

We must plan it, however, while we have her with us, I thought.

Of course the wedding of my earlier dreams was not possible. Nor did I want it. I had a guilty feeling that I had kept Steve—and the entire family—waiting too long. When I asked Steve about an immediate marriage, his joy and understanding removed any doubts.

My greatest surprise was when Grandma, with one of her crafty smiles, pulled out the little tin trunk and removed from it a beautiful cotton dress—white! Her only explanation was that she had felt since last Christmas that I would be needing one and had asked Father to get it for me! Could I doubt in any way that family of mine?

Also, Steve gave me a white satin-covered New Testament that he had found in his mother's precious possessions. I carried it instead of the usual flowers during the service and will treasure it always.

So, on New Year's Day afternoon, before the completed fireplace in the new home, with our minister Mr. Smither reading the services, Steve and I pledged our troth.

Grandmother, Father with Uncle Joe and his family, were seated around us. Mary and Marg with Paul Gray and Daniel Pound stood by our side. During the remainder of the day, groups of our friends came to drink a toast to the bride and groom.

Our life of togetherness had begun. I had not realized how happy I could be.

Steve had sold his home and moved the furnishings that we would want into a part of the new house. Grandma and Father were delighted that we could be at home and also by their side.

It was the Rangers' guns that tracked down the Indians and finally subdued them—the Rangers, that new fighting force which was growing into a standing army for the protection and welfare of our people. Other communities had not fared as well as ours. Our Republic was feeling the teeth of the resentment of the defeated army of Mexico as it worked with its handman, the Indian. We missed our friend, Neleetah! For peace had not been established at the Battle of San Jacinto.

Grandma was the calmest of us all during the following days. When she knew that Uncle Joe was under her roof again, she arose and prepared him a dish of gruel, creamy with butter. I found her sitting at his bedside when I called Father to his breakfast that next morning. The children were asleep in the trundle bed; Estelle in a chair by the fire.

Uncle Joe never returned to his home. The exposure, the excitement, and the unaccustomed early morning mist in his journey over to his old home gave him added pain and he seemed to grow steadily worse. In the days that followed it was we, who loved him most, who watched his intense suffering and administered to him to the last.

February ice had to be dug through to prepare his last resting place. The family burying ground was now established—that important, inevitable part of any pioneer's homestead. All of our pleadings could not persuade Grandma to remain at home. She went to the little schoolroom where Mr. Smither, the Presbyterian minister, came to soothe us in our bereavement. We rode in Johnnie's cart to the grave. Father's loving hands had fashioned the casket, but kindly neighbors did the rest. How different it was from the pine boxes Father used to make while I held a candle! And how long ago that seemed.

Afterward, Grandma sat by the fireside and greeted the friends who filed by her chair, their upset more evident than hers was.

The next morning we found that she had joined her son. We buried her beside him. My grandmother and Uncle Joe were gone, and without them our lives could never be the same.

Another Texas spring prevailed over sadness and loneliness of heart. Father and I clung to each other. I feared for him since I knew the emptiness of my own life. Yet I had Steve! Father stood like the stalwart man he was, but he was hard to reach in his double loss. It would be up to me to fill the vacancy to the best of my ability, to see that he never felt neglected. He and Steve worked hard on the completion of the new house—Father to occupy his thoughts, Steve with the incentive of ownership and the prospect of a family.

Steve and I now walk down the road together to find courage around the corner, to know the trials of paving a broader land, to meet the glories of success with humble pride, to enjoy the new country we are building.

I hope I do not fail in the purposes that come to me. I am young, yet old enough to realize the duties and the hardships that will be mine as a pioneer wife in Texas.

Yet, except for the loved ones who are now gone—although they are each and all a part of me forever—I would not want anything otherwise.